ALWAYS IRELAND

A NOTE ON THE AUTHOR

Roy Kerridge was born in 1941, and has lived since then in London and Sussex. After school he began writing articles for the *New Statesman,* for which he continues to write. As well as publishing many books, he has contributed to newspapers, journals and magazines, including a column for *The Independent* for nearly three years.

Roy Kerridge numbers among his hobbies drawing cartoons, going to gospel concerts and creative sleeping.

ALWAYS IRELAND

An Englishman in Ireland

ROY KERRIDGE

with Drawings by Musa

POOLBEG

For Richard West

First published 1993 by
Poolbeg Press Ltd
Knocksedan House,
Swords, Co Dublin, Ireland

© Roy Kerridge 1993

The moral right of the author has been asserted.

A catalogue record for this book is available from the British Library.

ISBN 1 85371 256 6

Cover illustration by Wendy Robinson
Inside drawings by Musa
Set by Mac Book Limited in Stone 10/15
Printed by The Guernsey Press Company Ltd,
Vale, Guernsey, Channel Islands

CONTENTS

Foreword by Mary Kenny   i

Introduction   iii

1   1969: The Crown Liquor Saloon   1

2   1973: In the Buttery   13

3   1982: Around the North   17

4   1988: A Journey to Dublin   26

5   O'Brien's Hotel   35

6   Koala Visit   43

7   A Kilmainham Look   50

8   Beautiful Dungarvan   69

9   On Fota Island   99

10   From Ireland to Wales   110

11   1991: Dublin and Belfast Diary   129

12   A Dolphin in Dingle   151

13   Anyone for Ennis?   160

14   1992: Dublin Again   177

ACKNOWLEDGEMENTS

I would like to thank the following individuals for their kind help and encouragement: Yukki Yaura, The Noble Wise One, George Lekaukau, Michael Wharton, Mr Chisholm, the coffee house waiters at the Grosvenor Hotel, Victoria Station, Anita Farmer, Sheila Ryan, Dora Thornton, Margaret Drage, Michael Kavanagh, Brian Behan, Anita Marie Bowers-Barnes, Nisa Khan, Eveleen Coyle, Cynthia Reid, Clawhammer Jones Bingo, Pauline Kiernan, Alex Mijakovac of Dublin, Brighid McLaughlin, Stan Gebler Davies who gave up his bed for me, and Jeffrey Klinke who gave me an unbreakable plastic bag from Jermyn Street.

AUTHOR'S NOTE

As some of the people I met in Ireland did not know I would promptly put them in a book, I have tried to lessen the shock by giving them fictitious names. Phil, Mr and Mrs Price, Regan, Eagan and Kiely are not the real names of the persons described. Some portions of this book have appeared in *Country Music World* and *The Independent*. I would like to thank the editors concerned, John Shotton and Andy Bull, for permission to reproduce this material.

FOREWORD
Mary Kenny

Roy Kerridge is one of the great characters of literary London—in true Dr Johnson and Bohemian tradition, rather than in the Beverley-Hill-style-big-bucks-deal image of the newer glitterati. Roy's unassuming appearance, his habit of carrying his personal belongings for the day in a plastic bag, his encyclopaedic knowledge of grass-roots Britain, and in particular, through his own family links (his step-father was African), of the Afro-Caribbean community, have all contributed to his very special reputation as an acute observer with an unusual background. Roy's upbringing, among the Biblically-formed black gospellers, has not only left him with an indelible love for gospel music, but with sensitive antennae for faith and spirituality, and sometimes, too, with a gentle, old-fashioned morality. But Roy never judges people moralistically, and he puts into practice that excellent counsel that a soft answer turneth away wrath: even when a Glasgow-Irishman, the worse for drink, yells abuse at this Englishman, Roy's response is to offer him a funny drawing to make peace.

Such incidents seldom occur, however, in Roy Kerridge's travels. He is naturally in tune with the character and atmosphere of Ireland. As a writer, he has a physical sympathy with the terrain, which is an important aspect of Ireland and Irishness: he sees and feels "the soft green countryside of small fields, with an occasional heron or peewit standing alone in the damp grass." He has an instinct for the psychic and the fanciful element in the Irish imagination, and glimpses, as it were, the wood-nymphs in the trees as he passes. He looks at how Irish people build their homes—and particularly their bungalows—in rural areas, and what statements this domestic architecture makes about the metaphorical (as well as the actual) value of land and its perspectives.

He reports conversations and songs and events in a way that gives us a snapshot of Ireland that is at once observational and appreciative. He has, especially, a touching affection for Dublin Zoo, which indeed is one of the most charming in Europe.

Perhaps because of his own unusual background, Roy Kerridge sees and understands, as few overseas writers have done, the spiritual character of Ireland and how deep that goes within history and tradition: never contentious or patronising, Roy has grasped the point that if you remove their faith from the Irish, you remove their historic soul. And yet he seems to affirm that because the Irish character has itself remained so paradoxically consistent, the personality of Ireland cannot be erased or occluded, for Ireland will always be Ireland. For the Irish, it must always be a pleasure to have Roy amongst us: the *ceád míle fáilte* will surely always be extended to him.

INTRODUCTION

Writing books about Ireland is a pleasant occupation. The last time I tried it, I sought to end with a flourish, and declared that when a High King ruled again from Tara, I would return to Ireland. I waited and waited, but all in vain. To my chagrin, it became plain that the Irish were not immediately going to restore their ancient kingship system. Swallowing my pride, I returned again and again to Ireland. When I wrote *Jaunting Through Ireland* in 1988, I imagined that most of my readers would be as English as I am. To my surprise, the most friendly book reviews came from Irish writers living in Ireland. So this time around, I am writing with both Irish *and* English readers in mind.

My first visit to Ireland took place in 1969, when I was twenty-eight years old, and very young for my age. I had read that, according to Bernard Shaw, nobody who goes to Ireland is ever the same again. Against all the odds, I had succeeded in living through the sixties as a young man without ever taking an illegal mind-altering drug. It seemed a pity to waste this achievement by going to Ireland and altering my personality after all. So I compromised, by going to the "safe" British part of Ireland—Belfast—where the hallucinogenic Shavian influences would, presumably, be absent.

Returning to England a bare three months before the Troubles broke out, I waited four years before I felt brave enough to go to the Republic. When I did so, I found myself in a land more easygoing and slower-paced than was the North of Ireland. I liked what I saw. Realising that I was bound to change whatever happened, I gave up bothering and returned to Ireland whenever I had the chance. On each occasion I kept a journal and later smoothed it down into essay form.

My early fear of the Republic of Ireland was not of violence but of succumbing to drink. I read the works of Brendan Behan with horrified fascination. Like many Englishmen of twenty years ago, I regarded Brendan as a typical Irishman. Last year (1991) I met a *real* typical Irishman of the present day. He lived in a suburban house on a new estate, mowed the lawn, washed the car and ate trendy dishes prepared by his wife in a stripped-pine kitchen. In England he would have been called a "*Guardian* reader." He might even have *been* (Lord save us!) a *Guardian* reader. Whatever he was, he was very kind to me and let me sleep in the best bedroom.

His name was Phil and he was a young engineer with a large family. When the children were in bed, one night, he told me tales of his earlier life as a first mate in the Irish Merchant Navy. In his untamed bachelor days, he had been a more rugged kind of Irishman.

"At the age of twenty-five I was alone on the bridge, in command of my ship. The end of freedom at sea came with so-called 'improved communications.' Instead of Sparks tap-tapping on his radio, we had phones installed, and any fool in the shipping office could ring you up no matter what ocean you were in, and pester you with some nonsense or other. So in the end I quit."

We compared notes on New Orleans, a favourite city of mine, where Phil had helped sweating dockers load cotton from the barges. After many stories of cunning thefts by dockers in a thousand "pre-container" ports, he gave me a harrowing account of how dockyard police at Mozambique used to beat up men for taking stale rice from seamen who would otherwise have thrown it away. In Chicago, my host and his fellow seamen had stayed in a wharfside "black quarter."

"When we had been there three weeks, drinking alongside the locals, a white American suddenly braked his car when he saw us and shouted 'Jump in, quick! Your life isn't worth a nickel out there!'"

Talk turned to schooldays, and I heard once more a familiar complaint about the cruelty and sadism of the Christian Brothers of yesteryear.

"I got caned *every day*, not for bad behaviour but for mistakes in my lessons. The lay teachers were nearly as bad. One teacher was so bad that I vowed I would beat him up when I left school. Suddenly, a year ago, I saw him in the street, and called his name. He cringed back, obviously expecting that I'd hit him, but he was so old and feeble that I hadn't the heart to touch him. So he got off lightly. Times have changed, sure enough. My little boy came home from school crying the other day and said, 'My teacher shouted at me.' *Shouted* at me—ye gods! When I was a boy it was a good day if the teacher only shouted at you. Now they're not allowed to use the cane."

Finally, Phil marvelled at the English ignorance of all things Irish.

"An English colleague came over here, an engineer like myself, and I drove him to Limerick. On the way, we passed some Irish Army tanks and Landrovers that'd been on an exercise. 'Is that the IRA?' the Englishman asked. Don't the English know *anything* about Ireland?'

"Of course they don't," I replied. "Not one Englishman in ten knows about the Border. When they hear news about 'Northern Ireland' on telly, they imagine it means the same as 'Northern England' at home—just a region, not a separate state. Partition hasn't yet sunk into the English mind. Most English people think the Troubles are happening all over Ireland—north one week and south the next—and they can't understand why British troops are involved."

This amazed Phil, and he bade me goodbye with a puzzled expression on his face.

1

1969: THE CROWN
LIQUOR SALOON

Seagulls cried and swooped, as the Liverpool to Belfast ferry boat ploughed a swirling white furrow through a dark blue sea. It was a bright spring day. Above me, on the bridge, the Union Jack billowed like a sail from the masthead. A pair of guillemots, black above and white below, flew side by side across the foamy wake. Their bodies were streamlined, but their wings whirred clumsily—partridges of the furrows of the Irish Sea.

Too excited to stay in one place, I made my way towards the lounge. Two gannets, like brilliant white arrows, streaked on a course parallel to the ferry boat. No doubt they hoped that the bottom-dwelling fish would be raised to the surface by the churning waters. Delicate patterns of jade green swirled within a sparkling comet of white froth.

Below deck, I paused for a glimpse of the steamy, fascinating engine room. Then I hurried down to the lounge, a brown place of ancient leather seats and settees, with tiny portholes and a cosy smell of stale beer. Here I had left my huge orange suitcase, once the property of my grandfather. It was covered in labels, such as P&O, Bombay. As I am of nervous disposition, I needed to make sure that it was still there.

A small band played, elderly pub musicians with a repertoire of music hall tunes, sentimental songs and comic ballads such as "The Irish Rover." Boozy house-wives swayed in their seats to the music of banjo, spoons, fiddle and accordion. Eight young girls, in bright clothes and with dyed hair, performed a rough and ready "knees up" dance, to my wonderment and delight.

From the bar danced a cheerful drunk, a glass in his hand, a brown hat on his head and his coat and scarf hanging loosely about him. Bawling above the music, he sang the Liverpool song, "Maggie Mae," the orchestra obligingly changing tune to follow him. So enraptured was I at all these carryings-on that I noticed our arrival in Belfast only when I felt the ship slow down and noticed other passengers searching for their luggage.

I hurried along with the crowd, wondering what would happen to me. Where was I to stay? A golden glare of sun showed that dusk was not far off. Helplessly, I put my suitcase down on Irish soil—or Irish concrete, to be more precise—and looked about me. Apart from the other passengers, I could see only incredibly fat ribald-looking dockers in thick jerseys. They sat comfortably on the cargoes of wood they were supposed to be moving, and gazed scornfully at the myriad passers-by. I could see that I would receive no help from that quarter.

A man in an official-looking cap and jacket soon attracted my attention. He too was a stout man, but he looked tremendously important, in his black-rimmed spectacles. Pointing here and there, with an air of owning the city, he gave instructions to lost travellers such as myself. Obviously, I thought, he was a chief customs officer or a harbour master. Timidly I approached him, noticing his green shamrock tie-pin with awe, and asked him if he knew where I could find a taxi.

"I am the taxi driver!" the man replied grandly. "Where is it that you want to go?"

"Er, I wanted a place where I could get bed and breakfast."

Pressing my nose to the cab window, I stared at the old-fashioned city whizzing by outside, noticing such painted slogans on the grey walls as "Prods Rule OK."

"What are all those writings on the walls?" I asked.

"It's the gangs—you know," he said, his face growing blank.

Soon we stopped outside an extraordinary yellow pub, The Crown Liquor Saloon. I went in to see if there were a vacancy for bed and breakfast, while the driver waited.

"Aye," the landlord nodded, so I collected my case and gave the taxi driver a two-shilling tip. Then I stared in astonishment at the ornate and wildly over-decorated Victorian pub. (Present-day note: The Crown Liquor Saloon, which no longer does bed and breakfast, is now the property of the National Trust. In 1969, it was still "natural.")

Evidently unaltered in seventy years, the Crown stood

Belfast City Hall

gilded by the evening sun. Decorative marble columns made a startling and vivid sight, shining yellow with touches of green and scarlet. Imitation vines, sculptured into the stonework, had been painted in more than natural colours. What with the mosaic tiles and swirly metalwork, the face of the Crown shone like a sun upon the crowded pavements of the dingy street.

In the dark interior, I signed a huge book and paid a week in advance for bed, breakfast and evening meal. A bald man with dull eyes took my suitcase and marched with it out of a side door into the street. Sleeping accommodation was outside the pub, across the road, in a semi-derelict side alley. The man plonked my case down in a black doorway, pointed up the narrow steps and gave me a key with a number on it.

Toiling up on my way, landing after landing, I said good evening to other guests who popped their heads out of doorways. A star-crossed young couple, who seemed to be runaways, looked me up and down in evident relief. I imagined that the young man resembled a slender pinch-faced Brendan Behan, with his curly hair and open-necked shirt. Three bulky gangster-like Chinese men in suits stared at me in querulous alarm when I reached my landing. Later, at dinner, they told me that they had come to Belfast to prospect for a Chinese restaurant. As yet, the Northern Irish were unaware of the delights of Oriental dishes.

My room was small and shabby, but I felt relieved to have a room at all. Stretching out on the creaking bed, I enjoyed a short nap.

During the week I stayed in Belfast, I relished every moment I spent in the bar of the Crown, making one glass of cider last an hour at a time.

Both outside and inside, it seemed as though a line had been ruled above the ground floor of the pub. Above the line was grimy brickwork and darkness. Below it was carefully designed beauty and elegance. The elegance seemed wasted, for all the thirsty customers were burly fierce-looking workmen, who gazed raptly at the television from beneath bushy black eyebrows. Their chins jutted out, their hands were enormous with veins like muscles, and they wore huge boots and dirty mackintoshes. Yet the pub was so fascinating that if it had been in London, every aesthete would have been there, twittering with joy.

Chandeliers hung from the ceiling, and all around the walls opposite the one long bar, facing the small tinted windows, were wooden "confession boxes." Each box had a swing door that led into a small enclave containing seats and a table. These enclaves, obviously meant for secret plotters, had settle-back oak walls but no roofs. Every few feet, along the chain of hidey-holes, stood an heraldic beast, erect as if in defiance—lions, eagles, griffins, unicorns and even bears. Each inch of dark oak wood was carved in detail. Flowers, nuts, squiggles and symbols curled and twisted lovingly around.

I liked to sit alone in a cubby-hole and soak up the soothing ecclesiastical atmosphere. Most of the other customers preferred to lean elbow-to-elbow against the bar, facing the telly. Dreamily, I would gaze at the windows, where sentimental Victorian cut-outs had been stuck to the glass. Prettily coloured robins, finches, blue tits and swallows fluttered around with cherubs and cupids, among roses, lilies and violets. Ignoring the far-off cries of "It's a goal!," I felt as if I might be in Heaven itself.

On my second day in Belfast, I stumbled upon a small bright procession of youths in orange sashes. They marched along to the crash of drums and the light, enchanting piping of flutes. Banners fringed with gold swung past. In the regalia of the Orange lodges, I caught an echo of army parades in London and the faded military colours hanging in English churches. Brighter and more light-hearted than soldiers, these youths might have stepped straight from the time of William of Orange, a time when Protestantism had been taken seriously in England. At the same time, some of the pavement foot-followers (so to speak) had a rough delinquent appearance and wore strips of Scottish tartan on their windcheaters.

Gradually, I found my way around the city, and spent much of my time listening to the brass band in the Botanical Gardens. An appreciative crowd would gather around the seasidey bandstand. Inside the hothouse, I would lounge beneath spreading palm fronds and chat to the gentle bearded young gardener.

From the bus station, I made many trips into the beautiful Ulster countryside. I saw the Giant's Causeway, supposedly constructed by Fionn Mac Cumhaill, the mythological giant. From the narrow ledge pathway, I looked up at the fluted patterns of the Giant's Pipe Organ and down at the neatly diced stone blocks in the sea, nature-carved squares with seagulls for chessmen. In the main square of grey old Bushmills, where they make the whiskey, I felt as if I were indeed in a foreign land, a place of romance and literal intoxication. Further south, towards Ardglass, I explored tiny fishing villages, where little cottages lined narrow streets that curved down to the sea.

From bus windows I gazed on a soft, green countryside of small fields, with an occasional heron or peewit standing alone in the damp grass. Clean white cottages of smallholders stood here and there among the fields. In one garden I saw a pump with no fewer than seven black kettles grouped around it. One day a bus took me through a small village dominated by the red brick of the Orange lodge, the tallest building there. It was four storeys high and top-heavy with it, leaning precariously out over the narrow road. Nearby, covering the whole side wall of a cottage, was an immense painting of King Billy (Prince William of Orange), the ruler who kept England Protestant at the end of the seventeenth century. The monarch was in characteristic pose, triumphant over Catholic foes at the Battle of the Boyne. By a twist of fate, the battle site is now in the Republic. In brilliant colour, William sat astride a white horse, a plume in his hat and a sword held aloft by a stiff elbowless arm. I was reminded of Cornwall, where gigantic Biblical texts are often painted on household walls by pious fishermen.

Later, I was to discover villages where virtually

everyone was Roman Catholic.

Back in Belfast, I admired the Queen's University, a stately home of learning with an immense iron gate. Nearby, in Botanic Avenue, I explored the haunts of students. In one coffee bar, a place with unnaturally bright white lights, I tried to engage some of them in conversation. They seemed inordinately fond of revolution, and might have felt more at home in the plotting chambers of the Crown Liquor Saloon.

"On holiday, are you?" a tall blond-haired young man asked loftily. "I daresay you think Ireland is full of little white cottages."

"Well, isn't it?"

"Yes, but there's more to it than that. We are on the verge of great social change, here. Up till now, the Catholics have been denied equal rights, in the areas of housing and government. They provide our civil rights movement, just like Martin Luther King in Mississippi. Look, we want a world revolution, right, or how do we get socialism? In America and South Africa, revolution will come from a race war. But in Ulster, revolution might come out of a *religious* war!"

"Take no notice of him," another young man interrupted. "Our struggle is for peace, friendship and fair play for minorities, not violent behaviour."

"Be that as it may, could you tell me the way to the River Lagan?"

"Why, have you got a canoe, or a yacht?" the first student enquired eagerly.

"No, I just want to see the river."

With a look of contempt, he took me to the door and pointed the way.

Soon, to my ecstasy, I was walking up and down the embankment of Belfast's famous river, below the over-hanging trees of Ormeau Park. The park railings adjoined the river promenade, and beyond them, wooded hillocks rolled away towards the nearby countryside.

As I walked, I happily sang one of the most poignant Irish ballads ever to be recorded by my hero, Lonnie Donegan—"My Lagan Love." Nobody else was about, so I did no harm. Swifts wheeled away from me in alarm.

Where Lagan stream flows to the sea,
There dwells a lily fair.
The twilight gleam is in her eye
And the night is on her hair.

At last I could see the fabled Lagan, possibly the "stream" mentioned in this traditional song. For some reason, all four songs recorded on the blue extended play record, "Relax with Lonnie," had a mystical significance for me as a young man. "Kevin Barry" was the song that made me interested in Ireland in the first place. "Bewildered," a bluesy soul-ballad, summed up my general frame of mind. "It Is No Secret," a hillbilly spiritual, actually had a hand in converting me to a belief in God. Just as most people believe in the First Christmas while they sing carols, so I found myself unable to disbelieve in God whilst hearing "It Is No Secret."

Such songs undid some of the harm caused by the

1950s' "skiffle movement." In skiffle days, young men modelled themselves on outlaw characters whose adventures were recounted in song by blameless balladeers. Nowadays, popular songs no longer tell stories. Young men who want to be bad model themselves on the real life characters of the *singers* instead.

Next day, I roamed along Bohemian Botanic Avenue and found myself at last in Sandy Row, the Protestant heartland. Rows of sturdy little terraced houses stood in compact chunks of "two-up, two-down," with ridges along the roofs to show where one home ended and the other began. The brickwork was grey and aged, but the doors, window-frames and doorsteps were scrubbed, bright and impeccable. In the net-curtained windows, decorations of various sorts made a fine display. Beyond the potted plants, toy animals and costume dolls, sweet little cottage interiors with vivid wallpaper could be glimpsed.

At the end of each row, the windowless end wall had become a scribbling pad for teenagers and children. In chalk and whitewash, they proclaimed their "religious" gang slogans and drew clumsy versions of William of Orange in *the* pose on horseback, with hat, sword and arm. Wild and neglected-looking children played everywhere. Could it be that the householders of Belfast held their houses neat and pretty at the expense of their children, whom they chased outdoors to fend for themselves?

One boy of seven or so, in grey ragged clothes, approached me holding out his hands. I could not understand his strong local accent. As soon as I stopped walking, a crowd of boys converged around me, all a few years older than the first boy. Of their two leaders, one was a fat, pasty, curly-headed child, with demented wire spectacles. The other was a tall bright-eyed boy with short, sleek hair, combed forwards. At first I looked at them benevolently, not realising what a novelty I was in the neighbourhood.

"Giss a *panny*, mister! Giss a *panny*!" the youngsters demanded vigorously, jostling one another.

I had only three pennies, so I handed them out and then tried to go on my way, with a seemingly nonchalant "Cheerio!"

But the kids were having none of it! Shouting, roaring and calling reinforcements from every corner, they milled after me, tugging at my clothes. At first I grew embarrassed, then frightened. Western tourists in an Arab bazaar or a Haitian market might understand my predicament.

Help was at hand, for a burly man in a cloth cap and black plastic mackintosh rode past on a bicycle.

"Away, ye spalpeens!" he commanded in a terrible voice, brandishing the back of a horribly knuckled fist. The children fled, the man on the bike rode on, and so I was back in time for supper at the Crown after all.

🍎🍎

2

1973: IN THE BUTTERY

In this auspicious year, I made my first visit to the Republic of Ireland. Disappointed at first by the shabbiness of Dublin, I cheered up when I saw the grey cobbled splendours of Trinity College. These were the heady days when undergrads thought they could overturn the world. What does my dog-eared old diary have to say?

May 1973

Today I saw an enormous bank that used to be the house of parliament before the Act of Union. Near here I found Trinity College, one of Dublin's universities. At one time, the university was reserved for sons of the Anglican Ascendancy.

While I was roaming around the quad, a bell must have rung, for students released from lectures burst from cloister-like doors and ran pell-mell across the cobbles into a basement bar, the Buttery. I followed them, and found myself in a crowded room full of smoke, beer fumes and students sitting around canteen tables shouting about politics. I ordered a Guinness and sat down, quickly drawn into the conversation. My companions were four tall wild-haired young men with innocent faces, and a spiritual-looking girl from Enniscorthy called Avril. I had the idea that most of the students still came from Church of Ireland backgrounds, but sought to conceal the fact.

"What's happening in the world?" I was asked, as if they were trapped in the Buttery and eager for news.

"Well, the war in Vietnam..."

"No! No! England, England! What's happening in England?" they all chorused.

"Well, my friend Ian Robinson has started a magazine called *The Human World* and I'm writing articles for it," I said modestly.

"A writer! Do you know RD Laing?" asked a hawk-nosed youth.

"No, thank you very much, and I don't want to, either. Isn't he the one who says we'd all be better off mad?"

"Yes, and he's quite right, d'ye see? It must be marvellous to be mad. Like being drunk all the time," he concluded dreamily.

"Is it worth continuing our studies, when there's going to be a revolution?" I was asked next, as if I were a sage.

"A revolution? Are you sure?"

"Oh yes, a revolution will sweep the whole West any day, and all our lives will be transformed."

All of them began to talk blandly about the revolution as if it were a magic spell that would change everything into something new, and better, without human agency. The students weren't *working* for a revolution, they were *waiting* for one.

"My friend Eugene is a *real* working-class revolutionary, and he's got links with the IRA," Avril told me, beckoning to a scrub-bearded boy with bleary blue eyes.

Eugene seemed of a grittier and more single-minded breed than the others. I decided he had begun life as a Roman Catholic and would probably return to his parents' fold once he had graduated from the Buttery.

"There's a lot of capitalism about nowadays, that's why there will have to be a revolution," he said, in dogged trade unionist tones. "I hope I can finish my course before then. I'm doing Business Studies."

Leaving the friendly students, I wandered off to Christ Church Cathedral, another Ascendancy haven. The red-brick houses in the streets around the great church were practically falling down, though inhabited. Wild children threw bricks around and tried to beg from me. Inside the cathedral, I saw a sad-eyed lion and unicorn sculpture, lying broken in the mediaeval crypt. Strongbow, the first Norman conqueror of Ireland, lay here at rest. In 1173 he had rebuilt Christ Church. The cathedral had been founded about a hundred and fifty years earlier by King Silkenbeard, the Christian Viking King of Dublin.

Not far away, I discovered another Anglican cathedral, St Patrick's, where Jonathan Swift of *Gulliver's Travels* fame had been dean. His "Tale of a Tub" is the best argument for Anglicanism I've read. The guide pointed out a floor-tile memorial to the dean's platonic love, Stella. "There was no hanky panky between them," he observed sternly.

Back at the Buttery, I found that most of the students had reached an RD Laingian degree of drunkenness and were crashing into tables and falling all over the floor. Avril was still there, misty-eyed but almost sober...

(*Here ends the night's entry in my diary.*)

3

1982: AROUND THE NORTH

"Write your full name and address in the book," the bearded hotel-owner told me. "Then if you're found dead, we'll know where to send the body."

With that, he laughed immoderately and I gave a wry smile, trying to see the joke. No, I had not taken a trip backwards in time to Tombstone, Arizona in the days of the Wild West. I had merely taken the ferry once more from Liverpool to Northern Ireland. Evidently, the Troubles had done much to encourage "graveyard humour," just as the lawlessness of the Old West had given rise to laconic cowboy humour a hundred years before.

In a mood of sad-sweet nostalgia, I retraced my steps of 1969, from Botanic Avenue in Belfast to the banks of the River Lagan, along Ormeau Road. On my earlier visit, I had not realised that the terraced streets near Ormeau Park formed part of a staunchly Roman Catholic neighbourhood.

"Brits Out. Viva Argentina. Provisional IRA!" proclaimed a large wall slogan in bright green paint. Paintings of Korky the cat and other cartoon characters mingled happily with Republican slogans on many a wall-end. Several houses were in ruins, showing the charred roof timbers now so typical of the city. Nevertheless, the streets bustled with life, and purposeful children scrambled everywhere. Some played war games, others nursed dolls, but all seemed quite independent of grown-ups. Gossipy housewives leaned on garden gates and world-weary men in dusty clothes sat on doorsteps.

Suddenly an army Landrover swung past, with a youth riding shotgun in the rear. More soldiers appeared in front of me. None of them seemed remotely menacing, and the lightweight rifles they brandished carelessly looked to me like toys made of black plastic. At this turn of events, the street perked up and became interested. Housewives looked up from their gossiping with expressions of deeply ironic amusement. A severe-looking young soldier with a pencil moustache took his stance at one corner, his gun pointing towards the pavement. To my surprise, a curly-headed little girl of three toddled over and patted the muzzle of his rifle. The soldier's face did not melt.

"Do you love John Paul II?" the child lisped.

"He's all right," came the cryptic reply.

Rough young men then appeared from surrounding alleys and doorways. Some of them approached the soldiers and stood glaring at them, thumbs hooked into the tops of their jeans. A rag-and-bone man, crying his wares, wheeled his barrow between the bystanders, and a coal lorry emerged from a side road just as the army were about to cordon it off with a long white tape.

Once on the right side of the tape, I turned and watched the soldiers opening car boots and peering into doorways. The ribald locals seemed determined not to take them seriously.

"You from England too, same as me?" I asked one soldier.

"Yep, I'm from Liverpool."

"Really? I was there when the Pope came. It was wonderful to see all the decorations, flowers, paper streamers and banners, covering whole houses. Unfortunately, the Orangemen came down from Everton afterwards and burned them all."

A look of incredulity came over the soldier's face, and I realised that he was the same man who had been approached by the little girl. He had probably heard quite enough about the Pope for one day.

🍎

In an attempt to unravel some of the mysteries of this new Belfast, I spoke to local youth leaders. One of them, a cocky young man, seemed bucked up no end by the news of West Indians rioting in London.

"We don't have your problems here," he said airily.

I felt more at home with a woman youth worker, who gave me a cup of coffee and explained that the Catholic and Protestant neighbourhoods had only

become clear-cut separate "kingdoms" in the early Seventies. "Before the Troubles reached their height, the streets and estates were mixed," she told me. "Then people began to move until almost every district was wholly Catholic or Protestant. Pressure was brought to bear by activists on those who wouldn't move, and some people were terrorised into leaving. But please don't judge Northern Ireland by Belfast. Take a bus out into the country, and you'll get a better picture of all of us."

At the bus station, I asked if I could go on a scenic tour and then decamp at the prettiest spot I could find, to look for accommodation as best I might.

"Don't do that," the clerk advised. "A girl did that last year, and she disappeared. When they eventually found her, she was sort of dead."

"Sort of *dead*!" I echoed thoughtfully, and bought a ticket to the seaside resort of Portrush.

Meanwhile, still in Belfast, I made ready to go and see the Orange parade on the twelfth of July. This is the anniversary of the day William of Orange defeated James II at the Battle of the Boyne in 1690. The parade lasts the entire day. Bands, led by mace-bearers, play Orange tunes such as the top favourite "The Sash My Father Wore."

Orange music is big business in Northern Ireland, and young and old spend a great deal of money on records and cassettes. In some shops, UVF records are obtainable. A group of vigilantes that opposes the IRA, the modern Ulster Volunteer Force has now grown to resemble its adversaries. You should never take the law

into your own hands, but try telling this to the UVF!
They might respond with one of their ditties, such as

Don't bury me in Erin's Fenian valley.
Take me home, in Ulster let me rest,
And on my gravestone carve this simple message:
"Here lies a soldier of the UVF."

The 1982 Orange parade seemed to be about three
miles long. Many of the fife, brass, accordion and pipe
bands came from Canada and New Zealand, the Scottish
diaspora. Boy and girl skinheads waving Union Jacks ran
up and down beside the brightly uniformed marchers. A
group of tall long-haired young men, opponents of the
parade, lurched drunkenly along terraced roof-tops
roaring abuse down at the crowds.

One of these young men, an unpleasant-looking
fellow (who resembled Mick Jagger), climbed down a
drainpipe to road-level and performed a derisive dance.
Then he bared his bottom to the crowds. An Orangeman
stepped briskly from the ranks, felled him with a clip to
the jaw, and carried on marching without losing step.
The Jagger lay unconscious where he lay. Pushed on by
the crowd, I could not ascertain his fate.

Punk and skinhead young teenagers danced alongside
the parade, through the suburbs and out into the country.
Uproarious groups of youths seemed to erupt from deep-
set lanes in the oak woods as they sought short-cuts to
the head of the parade. As drums and fifes played between
the oaks, I was reminded of old prints I had seen of the

American War of Independence.

"Joe Crow from Sandy Row," a stubble-headed boy sang, a new (and, alas, unprintable!) song for my collection.

&

Next day, after a bus ride through glorious scenery, I found myself in the Margate-like holiday resort of Portrush. In this Protestant resort, the holiday shows seemed to consist mainly of displays of hypnotism. In my bed and breakfast house, one of a seafront row, a portrait of the Reverend Ian Paisley graced the dining room. Some might call the good doctor an arch-hypnotist, others might claim him as the spiritual governor of Protestant Ulster. I have a somewhat grudging respect for the old charmer, who fearlessly includes his Belfast home address in *Who's Who*.

Late that night, I heard a girl outside my window singing the "Sash" in a pure sweet tone.

It's old but it is beautiful, its colours they are fine.
It was worn at Derry, Aughrim, Enniskillen and
the Boyne.

Portrush had obviously enjoyed its own Orange parade, for a triumphal red, white and blue arch still spanned a road near the ultra-modern amusement park. A line from the "Sash" adorned the wooden framework of the over-decorated archway. No one who has ever learned to sing this song can ever forget the tune. A Cork fisherman's song, "The Holy Ground" has a slightly similar air and less controversial words. So I tried to press the "Holy Ground," button in the jukebox of my mind.

Before returning to Belfast, I visited the ominous town of Portadown. At first, as I roamed neat Protestant streets and shopping terraces, I despaired of finding somewhere to stay. An aged flute-player greeted me as a brother when I dropped a coin in his hat and asked him about accommodation. "You don't want to pay a landlady; come and sleep on my floor," he invited me.

To his disgust I pressed on instead, and soon found a vacancy in a tiny white cottage on a side street with a Union Jack in the window.

Next day, I set out to look for the friends of a friend, a young couple who lived on a housing estate on the edge of town. Loyalist graffiti covered many of the walls of Portadown, and the name "Prowler" appeared again and again. At first, when I saw the slogan "I Was Here, by The Prowler," I thought I might have stumbled on a local oath-like expression, such as "I Was Here, by Thunder!" or "by Thor!" But no, "The Prowler" turned out to be an individual. When someone scribbled on his name, he returned in wrath, for he was a jealous Prowler.

"How dare you cross out my name! I put a curse on you. The Prowler," he had painted, in large admonitory letters.

When I reached the shabby brown-brick council estate, I found that the graffiti had become Republican.

Here the Pope was a hero, and "Brits Out" replaced the Union Jack. As in many parts of Northern Ireland, the Protestants lived in their own humble houses, while the Roman Catholics were council tenants. (Present-day note: this is no longer so widespread, and a prosperous Catholic suburbia has arisen in most places.) On the hilly recreation ground, a large Tricolour, the flag of the Irish Republic, hung from a lopsided pole whittled from the branch of a nearby tree.

Eddie and Katie Byrne welcomed me to their small but cosy house, and put the kettle on. A big, brown, dark-haired friendly man, Eddie had soon to leave for the snooker club. While he was away, vivacious red-haired Katie played me his tapes, for he is a local folk singer of note, and has made a cassette, "Ireland, O Ireland." It can best be described as Celtic mysticism meets the Baha'i faith, for both the Byrnes are Baha'is, followers of Persian Messianic philosophy.

"That makes no difference here," said Katie. "People ask 'Are you Protestant Baha'is or Catholic Baha'is?'"

Ireland, O Ireland!

4

1988: A JOURNEY TO DUBLIN

One fine day, I packed a big red, white and blue bag, put a plastic bag inside it, and set out for Dublin on a Slattery's coach from Paddington.

Luckily, I bagged a window seat on the coach. My neighbour in the next seat was a tall youth with a lone quiff of hair on his shaven pate. He had a pair of earphones on, and nodded his head to faint "tish"-ing music as if demented. A middle-aged man with glasses sat in front of me, also saddled with a young neighbour, a defiant-looking girl with dark hair. He tried to engage her in conversation.

"You young people have such opportunities!" he marvelled. "Are you studying, yourself?"

"No, I've been working in a hotel, but I've had enough of working."

Taking off his earphones, the youth beside me listened with interest. Soon it was quite dark. We would be travelling all night and arriving at Dublin in the morning.

After a motorway stop for refreshments, the youth and the defiant girl returned together, and asked the middle-aged man if he would mind moving. So he sat next to me.

"The young people have hearts of gold, but isn't it a pity there's no work for them?" he said.

"I don't know about hearts of gold, but those two seem to be getting along very well."

"Ah, you'll find the Irish people are very friendly."

In the seat in front of us, the youth was earnestly showing the dark-haired girl a book of his drawings and a sheaf of song lyrics he had written. He reached up to the rack and lifted down a guitar.

"Look at that moon!" said the middle-aged man, pointing out of the window. "It stands to reason there's a God. Who could have put that moon there if not God? I went on a pilgrimage to the Holy Land once— a wonderful experience!"

I wanted to ask the man if he had been a priest, but didn't know the Catholic terminology. He had the look of a man who had failed to become a priest through too great a simplicity. Finally I asked him if he had "ever been in the ministry."

"Yes, I've been in a monastery. I was with the Christian Brothers—that's a teaching order. But I wobbled. They used to be pitiless to those who wobbled, so I didn't stay a Christian Brother. It was a great pity."

Falling into musing silence, my companion brightened up when at another motorway stop, we saw a brown-cowled bearded monk eating uncouthly from a take-away carton. "Look, is that a Franciscan brother? Ah, how wonderful to have a Franciscan on board!"

Obviously, God wouldn't smite a coach with a Franciscan on board, so my good-hearted friend felt much safer. He told me of his pilgrimage to Knock, a shrine in County Mayo where Our Lady appeared. "It's wonderful there! Everyone puts hands on a stone wall and cries aloud!"

Not long after this, I fell asleep, waking suddenly at Holyhead. My companion was talking across the coach to a mild-eyed girl with long brown curly hair.

Sleeping streets of slate-roofed houses led down to the quay and the Dublin boat. We all emerged from the coach with our baggage and, after much queuing, found places to sleep on board the great ferry boat. Although it was one o'clock in the morning, there were plenty of other passengers. Some looked very much like travellers (who used to be called tinkers). One room had cinema-like rows of chairs, so I chose one and settled down for the night, the lights of Holyhead twinkling through the portholes.

Four years earlier, I had spent two days at Holyhead, a curious and gloomy little town entirely devoted to the Irish traffic. Perhaps in pagan days the holy head of the god-hero Bran had rested there, carried from place to place by his faithful warriors and eventually buried at Tower Hill in London, guarded by the ravens, the birds sacred to Bran. Despite having been severed from his body during a fight with the Irish, Bran's head kept its wits about it and talked continually. Anglesey, now linked to North Wales by the Menai Bridge, was once called Mona, the last home of the Druids and a place of secret pilgrimage for mediaeval students of the occult. Some of this strangeness, together with a lot of Irishness, had rubbed off on modern Holyhead. No ferry had been needed in Bran's day, for the god-hero had simply waded across the water to do battle with his Irish enemies.

Huge jagged black rocks by the sea had been painted with hooligan football slogans as if they were a council estate wall. Near here, the terraced streets had kerbstones painted red, white and blue, the sign of a Protestant neighbourhood in Northern Ireland. Holyhead's main street was a grey, sad little thoroughfare, sprinkled with tattoo shops and cheap Chinese restaurants. In the dusk, I set out to explore a jetty I could see, stretching out to sea, a lighthouse at the end.

At the edge of town, I came across a strange Gothic building with crumbling battlements behind a high wall. It was the Castle Hotel, where once the poet Yeats and Irish high society, Ascendancy style, had stayed in splendour when travelling to or from Dublin. Now it had fallen on evil times and advertised disco-dances. Enormous boulders, shovelled together, made a makeshift wall on the beach, where the jetty began. Despite the approaching night, I set out along the narrow walkway towards the on-off gleam of the lighthouse. My walk went on and on, for the jetty never seemed to end. After a time, far out to sea, it turned a sharp corner. Unwisely, I was walking along the parapet rim, the surging sea on one side and a barrierless fall down to a concrete path on the other. Unknown birds cried above my head in the night.

At last I reached the lighthouse, looked at it and turned back. A kindly moon appeared and lit my way back across the sea to the Gothic castle, which was now floodlit and booming with rock music. Dark mountains loomed behind the castle as, treading carefully, I walked along my narrow moonlit way through a surrealistic landscape.

Next day I hitch-hiked off into the countryside, found a village by a river and after exploring for a while, asked the local youth if there were a bus for Holyhead. Greatly interested by my accent, the young people stopped talking in Welsh, climbed down from the wall where they had been sitting, and asked me where I was from. None of them had been to London, and they listened wide-eyed to my tales of the Big City, before showing me to a bus stop.

Back in the present, a sudden movement told me that my ship was setting sail and that once more I was saying goodbye to Holyhead. That night there was a storm and the boat rose and fell alarmingly. I slept through most of it.

In the morning, all was calm and bright. On the floor beside me, a German boy lay asleep on his back, his arms stretched upwards in the air. Nearby, also on the floor, a young girl slept flat on her face. Many of the young people on board were Germans. A farmer in Pembrokeshire once told me that he had met a German youth hurrying for the Fishguard ferry, and had asked him why he was so fascinated by Ireland.

"It's the political situation!" the young man had replied.

The middle-aged man on the Slattery's coach had been disparaging of Germans. "Ah, now, they never mix at all. They buy farms and chain up the gates."

I went out on deck, and saw the mountains of Ireland in the distance, beyond the waves. Crowds sat in the bar, although it was closed, and gazed through the windows towards Dublin. When that city came into view, the girl with brown hair I had seen on the coach stood up and began to sing, pitching her voice into an archaic strange note, perhaps the ancestor of country and western singing. Her male companions listened appreciatively as she sang them back home.

She sang a fisherman's song, "When the Boys of Killybegs Come Rolling Home," and a jolly song with macabre words that I had first heard at a wedding in Tipperary, "Down by the Banks of the Suir." Fnally, just as we landed, she sang an Irish version of a song from Scotland.

Oh, the oak and the ash and the bonny rowan
tree,
They all grow green in the old countree.

Then she lit a cigarette and gathered her belongings. Descending the gangplank, I found myself in a dreary, industrial no-man's land and quickly hailed a taxi. Soon I was hurtling into the city, an uproariously cheerful

View of Dublin from the Liffey

young man at the wheel. "You wouldn't be asking car sixty-nine if I left my packet of fags on the back seat?" he shouted into his radio microphone.

"That's right, I wouldn't!" the reply crackled back, and he roared with laughter.

"Oh, hell with it," he said amiably as he drove straight through a red light and set me down outside Connolly Station. I knew my way from there.

The railway stations of Dublin have been renamed after patriots. Connolly is one of the two main stations, set high on a ridgeway above the streets. I crossed the road below the station and walked under the railway bridge into Talbot Street. This long street of little shops, growing less shabby as the station is left behind, is one of my favourite parts of Dublin. I stepped into a bank and cashed a traveller's cheque, assisted by a red-haired girl with a friendly smile, Celine Kavanagh. Soon I came to a crossroads and the road that crossed was Lower Gardiner Street.

On my previous visit to Dublin, in 1982, this road of tall Georgian houses had been exceedingly squalid. Litter lay everywhere, and Continental students sat in rows on the steps of ominous buildings advertising bed and breakfast. Now, like much of Dublin, Lower Gardiner Street looked more prosperous, almost genteel. The neon-lit pin-table arcades of Talbot Street had been closed, and the district had grown a fraction more respectable.

O'Brien's Hotel, advertised with a large sign, had a "vacancy for a single," and so, at long last, I had a place to lay my weary head. Tomorrow I would see Dublin!

Just now, sleep was of the essence.

5

O'BRIEN'S HOTEL

O'Brien's Hotel was a soothing, cathedral-like haven in which to recover from the rigours of my journey. A ponderous mahogany-dark Victorian interior of tall mirrors, hat-stands, rococo-florid ceilings, niches with vases and marble statuettes of draped females had been renovated in Indian restaurant style. Veneered plywood partitions, new walls bisecting rose ceilings, digital clocks on each landing above the statuettes, non-stop loudspeaker pop music and crimson flock wallpaper combined with original Victorian mustiness to make a unique atmosphere. People of almost any background, including Swedes, Turks, Arabs, Americans and Indians, seemed perfectly at home in hushed, genteel and creaking O'Brien's Hotel.

How a place could feel hushed and echoing when it was full of guests with loud music playing was an O'Brien's mystery. Whatever indignities had been visited upon the house, it never forgot that it had been built as a gentleman's residence in 1840. The gentleman still seemed to be at home, so the guests were on their best behaviour.

During my stay in Dublin, I grew more and more fond of O'Brien's. My bed was high off the ground, my dresser a complicated pyramid of curved drawers, movable mirrors and detachable handles. From my tall window I looked out on faded brick hotels and a road full of purposeful traffic hurrying towards the city centre.

On my first morning at breakfast in O'Brien's I took my seat in the vast faded plushness of the dining room with its gilt-framed oil paintings, and ordered black coffee from a sympathetic middle-aged waitress who looked like a kindly nun. "It's sunny out, but it's wild," she informed me, meaning "windy."

Sometimes, on my journey to or from my top-floor room, I would unexpectedly come across the silent waitress. She would smile and vanish into a doorway, perhaps to change the sheets and do the work of a chambermaid.

Restored by coffee, I strolled out into shop-lined Talbot Street. The long, shabby thoroughfare was just as long but a lot less shabby than it had been on my previous visit to Dublin. Neon tawdriness had been replaced by cheerful workaday respectability. A baker's shop even had currant buns on sale, my staple diet since boyhood but hitherto unobtainable in Ireland. They were labelled "London buns."

Talbot Street leads on to wide grandiose O'Connell Street, which is the Strand, Regent Street or Broadway of

Dublin. Before Independence it was called Sackville Street, a thoroughfare celebrated by Oliver St John Gogarty in the book with the ballad title, "As I Was Going Down Sackville Street." Statues, trees and fountains stretch along the centre of the street, a halfway mark for those crossing to the General Post Office of patriotic fame.

On my 1982 visit to Dublin, I had befriended two boys, aged six and seven, who were begging in a doorway in Talbot Street. Perhaps they were travellers. Both boys had begun their begging day by smearing their faces with grime. Instead of bowls or hats, they were holding out plastic take-away cartons for alms. To my surprise, I encountered the same boys on a Sunday, scrubbed pink and dressed to the nines. Their stern mother, wrapped in a tartan shawl, was dragging them firmly to Mass. Loftily, they ignored my greetings.

Child beggars now seemed rarer in Dublin, except for the babes in the arms of young mother-beggars. Traveller women with babies still wore plaid shawls, and now congregated at O'Connell Bridge over the River Liffey, holding out money-baskets. The tourist season was in full cry, and this made fashionable Dublin seem witless and feverish. Everyone was young, chirpy and Continental. Where was the Dublin of which I had read, with its sharp-tongued old women in black shawls, elderly drunken clerks holding forth in darkened snug bars, failed poets from the provinces and ancient crones named Dicey Riley sipping stout? Gone, all gone—vanished before the knapsack invasion of youth.

I crossed the busy street to pay my own respects to

the post office and cash a traveller's cheque. Halfway over, I stood beneath a monument to William Smith O'Brien (1803-64) which towered above me with folded arms. According to the inscription, he had been Sentenced to Death for High Treason in 1848. The sentence had evidently not been too effective, since O'Brien had lived on for a further sixteen years. Did he have any connection with O'Brien's Hotel?

Soon I was inside the great grey General Post Office, a soothing abode of peace and postal orders, with something of the air of a national shrine or war memorial about it. Brown wooden pillarboxes stood inside the building, with quaint lettering above the slots. There was a lot of shiny marble and mosaic, as well as a statue which depicted a dying warrior being pecked by a raven. At the time I surmised that the warrior was England, beaten down by the Great War, and at the height of his woes being molested by the Bird of the Celts, a carrion feeder which seeks out the weak and the dying. However, I later discovered that the warrior was Cúchulainn, the bloodthirsty Ulster hero of legend, slain by Queen Maeve's champion. The bird was not a raven but a crow, symbol of the war goddess Morrigu. Earlier, the Morrigu had appeared to Cúchulainn as the Washer at the Ford, scrubbing garments forever soaked in blood. Cúchulainn had recognised the garments as his own. Since Cúchulainn is supposed by many scholars to have been a Scouser from Merseyside, my first guess had not been entirely wrong. Beneath the statue was inscribed the proclamation read aloud to the bemused crowds when

Pádraig Pearse prematurely declared an Irish republic on Easter Monday 1916: "We declare the Rights of the People of Ireland to the Ownership of Ireland, and to the Unfettered Control of Irish Destinies, to be Sovereign and Indefeasible..."

These big words were mockingly read by the crow of Cúchulainn, for Destinies Unfettered can be wayward things, apt to fall under the control of the Morrigu.

Fortunately the General Post Office and Dublin itself have been repaired since the heady days of 1916. Unfortunately for me, the clerk refused to cash my traveller's cheque since I did not possess a passport or a driving licence.

"No wonder they shot the place up in 1916. I've half a mind to do the same thing myself," I muttered.

"What was that?"

"Nothing, nothing."

A nearby bank solved my problems, and I set out to see once more another Dublin landmark, Trinity College. It was holiday time, and the college's promenades catered for tourists, not undergrads. I walked around them, trying to imagine the wits and scholars of eighteenth-century Dublin. In the Bodleian-type library, I renewed acquaintance with the eighth-century *Book of Kells*. It is kept under glass and a new page is turned every day. Winged cows and cross-winged angels are my Kells favourites. Today the open page showed an Irish Christ with aggressive blue eyes, long rebellious blond hair and querulous eyebrows. He seemed the very soul of Ireland.

Leaving Trinity, a university founded by Elizabeth I,

I walked up the street to St Stephen's Green. In the late-Victorian heyday of the Ascendancy, St Stephen's Green was the Park Lane of Dublin, a place where you walked beside a long lake in the hope of meeting and greeting someone you knew, with rustlings of silk and raising of toppers. By 1973, it had become an alarming place, where hippie drug addicts were floundering in the bushes and the Georgian streets outside crumbled before the onslaught of decay and bulldozers. Now all was well once more in the park. Ducks quacked peacefully, and I sheltered from a sudden shower beneath the trees. The sun returned and gleamed on the windows of restored Georgian dwellings outside the park railings.

I admired a grey statue, "The Three Fates," a suitably Celtic theme even though the sculptor was German. It had been a gift from West Germany to the people of Ireland as a reward for "all their help after the war of 1939-45." What had the Fates in store for Ireland now?

On that fateful day in 1916 when the General Post Office first flew the Tricolour, the lawns of St Stephen's Green were a scene of great activity. Countess Markievicz, a leading rebel, was digging trenches in them. A forceful, haughty beauty of Ascendancy stock, the Countess had been a Gore-Booth before marrying a Polish nobleman. Brendan Behan's mother Kathleen, in her amusing autobiography *Mother of All the Behans* (Hutchinson, 1984), gives a vivid picture of the trench-digging Countess.

Apparently the fiery rebel spent much of Easter Week dressed in the costume of a Boer warrior. Nowadays, when fashionable Dublin is given over to Mandela-worship, it is forgotten how much the Boers meant to the Irish rebels of an earlier day. Both in England and in Ireland, "progressive" people championed the Boer farmer against the gold-digging Briton. Many Irish nationalists saw their own struggle and that of the Boers as part and parcel of the same fight, a righteous war of mystic peasants against industry and big business. Conservatively minded writers such as GK Chesterton and Hilaire Belloc became fervent pro-Boers and somewhat less fervent champions of Ireland. If I had lived in those days, without the foreknowledge that South Africa and Ireland were not fated to be rural lands of contented peasants, I might have become an Irish rebel and a pro-Boer myself. Few people in Britain considered the fate of African tribesmen. Kipling tried to see the Boer War as a war against whips and African slavery, but he over-estimated the idealism of Empire.

"Anyway [according to Kathleen Behan] as soon as the Rebellion started, she was out there in her Boer uniform—which consisted of an immense floppy hat and a green tunic and skirt. She started to dig a hole in St Stephen's Green, to defend it against assault by the Brits. Now, although there was all this fighting going on, many people were trying their best to ignore it and go on working as usual. Near her dug-out were some men working on some scaffolding, and they started to jeer at this mad woman in uniform digging a hole in the middle of a park. In the end she couldn't stand it any longer, and loosed off at them with her pistol, which she carried with her. They didn't stay at work after that."

I too left St Stephen's Green. After taking refreshment in a shady café, I returned to O'Connell Street and waited patiently at the bus stop marked "Zoo." Visiting zoos is one of the great pleasures of my life and Dublin's Phoenix Park Zoo is nearly as old and as famous as the zoo at Regent's Park. It was founded in 1839, two years after London Zoo first opened.

"Lord love us, it's taken long enough!" a woman exclaimed as the bus arrived.

6

KOALA VISIT

I sat upstairs in the bus and looked out at Dublin. In Mountjoy Street, a faded Georgian neighbourhood, the ancient lamp posts were a-twirl with circular cast-iron ornaments and hung with yellow signs reading "Koala Visit." Dublin was celebrating a birthday, as some high-up person had decided that the Vikings had founded the city as a safe house for dividing loot exactly a thousand years ago. Consequently, all kinds of touristy things were going on. The koalas, I decided, must be an Australian hurling team.

Dublin seemed a soothing, if seedy, Victorian city. My bus drove through leafy nineteenth-century terraced suburbs, where steps led up to hall doors, the ground floors having steep sloping lawns in place of basement "areas." I was reminded of the boarding houses of Bon Accord in Aberdeen.

Soon I was in the Phoenix Park, trotting along beside the garda (police) headquarters in a mood of keen anticipation. On my first visit to Dublin, I had met a very old man, tall and scrawny, who stared through the garda railings at the vast parade ground as if hoping to see ghosts of yesteryear.

"When we were part of Victoria's Britain, this square was full of marching men, buttons polished and brass bands playing!" he told me. "Now, with this lot in charge, the barracks is a half-dead training college run by bureaucrats who go home at half past four each day."

The Phoenix Park seemed unchanged since the Seventies. There was the same sunken square, with steps and railings that contained nothing at all. Probably a statue of Queen Victoria had once stood there. At the entrance to the zoo, I recognised the same old mock-Tudor hut with its yellow thatched roof, the oldest building in the zoo.

To my amazement, crudely drawn posters advertising koala bears were everywhere. So there *was* a real koala visit! A family of koalas had been loaned to Dublin by San Diego Zoo. Long ago I had resigned myself to never seeing a koala bear, and here they were in Dublin! A stately home near Dublin boasted a large eucalyptus grove, full of the bears' favourite leaves. If the koala visit had taken place in the animal-loving Fifties, Dublin Zoo would have been the centre of a koala sensation. Television documentaries have over-egged the nature pudding.

The Phoenix Park is a garden zoo, a delightful flowery place laid out around a long lake. From one side of the lake, steps lead up to a tall embankment where cages stand among trees and blossoms, with views across the zoo and the park outside. On my last visit, I had looked across the water to a paddock where stood a black shire horse without a head. It walked slowly around, with a faintly nonplussed air. Suddenly it stood upright and I saw that it was not a headless horse at all, but a gigantic bull-necked gorilla. On all fours, its thick black limbs resembled shaggy shire legs, and its head was invisible from afar, sunk between its shoulders. Now, in the same paddock, three young gorillas chased playfully around.

In great excitement, I followed the arrows towards koala-land. They led towards the old red brick lion house, another relic of the Victorian zoo. Dublin had once been famous for its lions, which bred prolifically and supplied lions to the zoos of the world, including Africa. Something about the mellow old lion house appealed to the beasts. Although they had been housed in small barred cages, outdoors and indoors, they had not repined, for in the wild lions lounge lazily around beneath the same tree all day and stir themselves only when they get hungry. By the time I made my first visit to Dublin Zoo, the lions had been moved to a large grassy enclosure on the far side of the lake, and leopards had taken their place in the lucky old house as great breeders. On my second visit, ordinary leopards had been replaced by rare clouded leopards with beautifully patterned black spots suffusing outwards as if painted in wash on the soft fur. These too throve mightily.

All the big cats had now been dispersed, and the barred cages had been replaced by a long well-lit

showroom of eucalyptus leaves and branches tied onto stumps. The house was far too big for the little bears, but at least it hadn't been pulled down, as was the fate of London Zoo's fine old Victorian lion house. I peered around, looking for koalas. Would they too become champion breeders, or did the fertility charm work only for cat-animals? A young woman keeper removed a bunch of eucalyptus leaves and revealed a fluffy, portly koala bear sitting on a branch. One of my life's ambitions had been realised.

The innocent cause of all this jubilation looked around with petulant little brown eyes. Soon the koala's expression changed to one of indulgent good humour as it caught sight of another clump of eucalyptus leaves. Seldom have I seen such expressive eyes. Human beings clearly played no part in the bear's scheme of things, and none of its looks was directed at the audience. Slowly and deliberately the koala climbed towards the leaves, and then began to browse, eating the leaves straight from the clump without using its hands. These hands, white with shiny black claws, gripped the branch firmly. The koala is not really a bear, but a unique tree wombat, from Australia.

Then an absurd well-fed expression crept over the bear's face, reminding me of an old-time alderman at a mayoral banquet. The bear's mouth began directly below its black button nose, like that of Dennis the Menace in the *Beano*. It was a pudgy ball of fluff, wearing a chinchilla fur of soft shimmery grey ruffling into white. Hands, feet and tummy were pure white.

Suddenly another koala bear popped out of the leaves and looked around with an enquiring alert expression, just as if it had been in the wild. The two bears hugged each other and touched noses. As they sat side by side, the first bear began to nod off to sleep, its eyes closing in a snoozing self-satisfied curve. They were not the only teddy bears in the zoo, for in a nearby cage, a baby tamarin monkey, obviously an orphan, clung to a toy teddy and gazed back at me with a forlorn expression.

Big cats had not been banished altogether, and I admired the heavy-headed jaguars and the Persian leopard with his soft white underbelly. In the cafeteria, I bought some kiwi fruit. On my first visit to Ireland, apples and bananas were the only fruit on sale. Now Ireland sold fruit that was almost unknown in England, such as the kiwi. I didn't dare eat them, but threw them over the moat into the rocky chimpanzee den. An old grey chimpanzee broke the brown kiwi fruit open and solemnly ate the bright green flesh inside. A bridge crossed the lake, where weeping willows gave shade to flamingos, pelicans and ducks. Two old ladies with very expressive faces looked at the birds for a moment and then began to complain of the high price of duck eggs. I crossed over to see how the black bears were getting on. The five merry little cubs I remembered had now grown up into big lumbering bears, skilful beggars who stood on their hind legs and snapped successfully at the buns that hurled towards them.

I sensed the warmth in the harsh Dublin accents of the crowd. Slight young men walked arm-in-arm with large stout women. Children climbed cheerfully over barriers and back again, and everyone fed the animals. The two old ladies stared with interest at the pumas. "Ah, they never let these ones out, they're so dangerous," one of them said.

At the African Plains exhibit, hidden moats gave the illusion that elephants, giraffes, zebras and hippos were all sharing the same stretch of savannah. A giraffe, patterned all over with a rich brown crazy-paving design, stood with its head and neck flattened against a tree, cropping the leaves. Seen against the soft Irish pastel greens of grass and bushes, the black and white zebras looked particularly attractive. Farewell, Dublin Zoo.

7

A KILMAINHAM LOOK

Over a soothing toast and black coffee breakfast in O'Brien's Hotel, I scanned a map of Dublin, trying to work out the easiest way to get to the suburb of Terenure. My mother's oldest friends and neighbours, the Kennys, had cousins who lived there, and I had a friend called Joan who lived in the same district. So off I went to Terenure.

Near St Stephen's Green, I noticed several robust young men sitting in doorways drinking from cider bottles. They seemed to be apprentice tramps.

On the other side of the Grand Canal, I found myself among the gardens and mellow Georgian dwellings of Mountpleasant Avenue. Near here was Richmond Hill, where I found a lass of Richmond Hill getting married in a church with a huge green dome. Green squares, surrounded by elegant houses, led me astray for a while. Eventually I shook myself out of my dream of admiration and trotted briskly towards suburban drives, avenues, closes and crescents. A copper beech branch reached out and biffed me on the head.

Rubbing my head, I was then confronted by two savage Jack Russell terriers. An old man ran across his lawn, called off the dogs and shook his fist angrily at the tree. "I've complained about that tree a hundred times," he shouted. "It looks all right, but then it gets you! But if I saw a branch off, then I'll be in jail."

Finding that I was English, he told me that he once had worked at Leicester. "Everyone treated me fine," he said. "But I wouldn't go back, not with all that IRA stuff going on. I couldn't show my face."

"No one would blame *you*," I said.

"No, I couldn't go to England, knowing what Ireland's done."

So the Troubles, which keep the English out of Ireland, also keep the Irish out of England. The kindly old man showed me the way, and soon I was knocking on the front door of Fergus and Margaret Regan, a middle-aged couple who didn't know me from Adam. They had bought their house from the Corporation, I learned, and had erected a smart new front porch.

"A friend of Tony and Eileen, is it? Come in, come in!" said Mr Regan, a smiling white-haired man in shirt-sleeves. Margaret, his equally pleasant-looking wife, asked me if I wanted tea. Their daughter bade me hello-goodbye and after she had gone, I was shown her wedding album and recognised photos of my London friends.

"How do you like your egg?" asked Mrs O'Brien.

"Egg? I asked only for tea."

It turned out that tea meant high tea, a delicious spread with fried egg, fried bread, bacon and sausages. Before long the couple were repeating the words of the copper beech man. "I could never go to England now," Mrs Regan sighed. "Not after what happened to all those poor soldiers. I could never look the English in the eye. I'd feel so guilty. IRA is it? They're animals—no, worse than animals." Being told that no one in England would blame them seemed to make matters worse, as if coals of fire were being heaped on their heads.

"My two brothers were killed in the British Army, one at Dunkirk and one in the desert," Mrs Regan added. Murmuring condolences, I looked down at my clean plate. Somehow it seemed all the more tragic to die for a country that was no longer yours. We sat in the bright kitchen annexe to a brightly polished and decorated front parlour. Learning that the couple had once spent a holiday in Plymouth, I brought up the subject of Dartmoor, as an excuse to tell some ghost stories of the moor.

"Ah, you want to go to the West of Ireland for stories!" Fergus exclaimed with relish when I had finished. "There's marvellous storytellers there. You see some old fellow in the pub holding them spellbound, and the other men nodding 'That's true!' and 'Ah, yes. That's right.' They'd scare the daylights out of you, if you had to walk home in the dark. They tell of the banshee. Now the banshee appears to people with 'Mac' in their name, like Macneath. She goes up to their window, combing her long hair, and all of a sudden she starts squayling, like!

That means one of the family is going to die.

"Now up on a hill here, there's a ruined house they call the Hell Fire Club. Men used to sit up there at night, playing cards. One man laid down the winning hand. They looked, and he had a club foot. It was the devil! By God, they ran out of there!"

Soon Fergus was telling me about wakes he had attended as a young man.

"Ah, they'd carry on drinking there for weeks! Wakes are much shorter now, it's going out. I remember the lads would tie a string around the dead man's neck, pull it and make him sit up!"

"That's shameful," his wife murmured, shocked.

David Thomson, in *Woodbrook*, mentions such customs, and assumes that they are dying out. However, my friend Christina Lowry, the vivacious wife of the rock'n'roll cartoonist, warmly defended wakes with strings attached and said that they still took place in her native Galway. She told me, on my return to England, that a dead man ought to be seen to be enjoying himself. Then she described a wake where the deceased, as his last request, had asked to be sat up at table with a glass of porter in front of him. This was done, and everyone made merry around him. However, someone else had to drink his porter.

Listening to the conversation, I grew fonder yet of the Dublin accent. With lots of hand-shaking, and amid cries of "God bless you, I'll see you again, please God," I left the home of the warm-hearted Regans and walked over to the house of my spirited friend, Joan Barry.

I had met Joan Barry years before, when travelling by train from Sussex to London. She had admired a painted stone that I was taking as a gift for the Features Editor of the *Daily Telegraph*. At that time, I painted pictures on stones, varnished them, and sold them in souvenir shops. At Victoria, I bought Joan a peach from the fruit stall, and she gave me a medallion of the Virgin Mary on a chain.

According to a leaflet she gave me, the miraculous medal, which I held in my hand, had the power to protect the wearer against evil thoughts and acts, grant indulgences and grant entry into heaven. The Virgin Mary herself had ordered it to be made on the day in 1830 when she had appeared to Sister Catherine Labouré, a young novice in a Parisian convent. (Later, I gave my medal to my sister Amina.)

Joan Barry also told me of her hero, Frank Duff (1889-1980), the founder of the Legion of Mary. A man of boyish enthusiasm, Frank Duff was not trained in the priesthood, but had followed his parents into the civil service in Dublin. In 1933, he left his job and thereafter devoted himself entirely to Legion matters. After working with Catholic associations that sought to help the poor, he became convinced that Mary, symbol of pure womanhood, had entrusted him with the task of rescuing girls from a life of prostitution. He and his followers, mainly strong-minded church-going women, opened hostels and persuaded girls to leave their bully-boy protectors and seek sanctuary beneath the banner of Mary.

Nowadays it is fashionable in England to laugh at men who try to rescue prostitutes. Their motives are called into question. Perhaps from America, where the Western "whorehouse" and its golden-hearted madam have become part of the nation's folklore, has come the idea that prostitutes lead happy lives of unending jollity. Reading the works of Frank Duff is a useful corrective for those who glamorise the prostitute's life.

"Ah, come in, will you?" shouted Joan Barry, when I tentatively knocked at her door.

As forceful and flashing-eyed as ever, she soon whipped me up a salad with kiwi fruit, as she told me of her latest Legionary adventures in Amsterdam and Nicaragua. For the first time in my life I tasted the delicious green flesh of a kiwi fruit, an exotic emerald gooseberry-plum I shall always associate with Ireland. The brown furry outer skin scarcely hints at the treasures beneath. Greedily concentrating on the kiwi fruit, I listened to snatches of Joan's conversation.

"Have you heard, there's a dangerous cult called Born-Again Christians?" she enquired.

"In England they're not considered a cult," I faltered, for Born Agains are now almost the only believing Christians left in Britain, and I am obliged to embrace them, Born-Again warts and all.

"England! What about the Gibraltar shootings? Ha! Before you leave Dublin, you must go to Kilmainham Jail. That's where many of the rebels against English rule were held prisoner and shot. It's a museum now, open on Wednesdays and Sundays. Now, let me show you my

Legion of Mary literature. You may have this book, *Baptism of Fire*, by Frank Duff."

I put the book in my plastic bag, with thanks, and looked around at the holy pictures on the walls.

"Can you explain the cult of the Sacred Heart to me?" I asked, seeing a picture of Jesus with His heart outside His body.

"Yes, the heart shown outside Our Lady and her son shows all that they've suffered. Mind you, when I was a wee girl, I'd say, 'There's a picture of Our Lord and Our Lady with their souls outside their bodies."

I wondered if her childhood belief had more truth in it than she now supposed. Cave paintings sometimes show bears or elephants with their hearts outside their bodies and arrows aimed at them. Perhaps the animals wear their hearts and souls on their sleeves to make it easier for others to possess them. Christian pictures often depict themes well known to pagan artists of old, copied again and again, their origin forgotten.

"The robin pulled the thorns from Christ's brow, and its chest was stained red with His blood," Joan Barry told me, as the merciful bird alighted on her lawn.

After a long excited chat, we both set out for the bus stop, as Joan too was heading for the town centre. Night had fallen. We sat upstairs and she gave me a commentary on the city, crossing herself whenever we passed a floodlit church. "I can't stand these modern buildings! Ah now, there's Dublin Castle, all lit up. Look, see that funny-looking statue of a woman out there on O'Connell Street, in the fountain? Some foreign sculptor

gave her to Dublin, to commemorate the city's thous-
andth anniversary. The wits of Dublin have named her
Bidet Mulligan, the floozie in the jacuzzi. Here's our
stop. Come on!"

Searching me up and down with fiery eyes and
evidently coming to a half-satisfied conclusion, Joan Barry
shouted a Legion of Mary farewell and was off to her
Legionary meeting. In a Chinese restaurant, I pored over
the literature she had given me. Everything written by
the hand of Frank Duff suggested goodness, courage,
simplicity and sympathy for the young women he
attempted to rescue. Some were raucous and drunken,
others were saints in the making, all were different and
each was individually appreciated by Frank Duff. With
the help of the police, he and his Legion succeeded in
closing down Dublin's historic red-light district, Monto.
This came as a shock to me, as hitherto I had read of
Monto only in tattered collections of Irish ballads, where
it was treated as a place not of tragedy but of rich comedy.

In *Baptism of Fire*, Frank Duff chronicles the last days
of Monto, and repeats the story of the devil at the card
table, evidently half-believing it to be true. This time the
devil was at Monto, and his suddenly noticed cloven
hoof caused a stampede for the card-house door. In
Ireland the Legion of Mary have done great work, but I
have doubts about the organisation's effectiveness in far-
off lands with unsympathetic governments. Still, the
Legionaries clearly enjoy travel. I wish them well,
particularly as one of their number has now introduced
me to the kiwi fruit.

On Sunday morning I set off for Kilmainham Jail, which my map of Dublin showed me to be far out from the city centre, a little way up a hill near the banks of the Liffey. In O'Connell Street I was surrounded by jovial hurling fans, on their way to see the All-Ireland final (Tipperary versus Galway). Their multicoloured flags added gaiety to the scene.

I sauntered along Bachelor's Walk by the side of the river. Smart big shops gave way to small decrepit shops and then to boarded-up ruins. Steps hewn from granite blocks led down the embankment to the swan- and seagull-haunted water. Soon I arrived at the Ha'penny Bridge, a tall, slender curved bridge with high railings. It resembled a half-set sun over the water. In 1973, I had found a dingy little flyblown café near the river here. Sitting down, I was surprised when a large plate of evil yellow-green soup was slammed unasked-for on the table in front of me. Everyone there had a set lunch, plonked down automatically by a stony-faced waitress, and it began with soup. At the time, I had escaped from the café and thought myself lucky. Now I felt nostalgic for it but couldn't find it.

Instead, I crossed the bridge, passed through an archway, and found myself in a cobbled Bohemia of old narrow Dublin streets. Traveller women in shawls begged with their babies in the doorways of antiquarian bookshops. Continental and American young people in large noisy numbers spoiled the atmosphere. Hard Rock Café-like restaurants with burger buns and booming music marred otherwise perfect alleys and byways. I recrossed the Ha'penny Bridge and vowed to explore Dublin's Bohemia when the tourists had gone home.

Jaunty Bachelor's Walk gave way to workaday Ormond Quay, as I walked alongside the silver Liffey past bridge after bridge. Grand buildings of Victorian days stood everywhere, now put to various purposes.

In time I reached the castle-like entrance of Kilmainham Jail, where rebel hunger-strikers had been forcibly fed during the Troubles. Hunger-striking seems to be part of the Indo-Celtic inheritance. In India, someone with a grievance appears at the doorway of the person who injured him. There he sits, refusing to eat, in ash-strewn mourning. His presence is an alarming reproach to the supposed wrongdoer, who does not want blood on his hands. Usually the wronged party, in Indian villages, is given some restitution to make sure that he goes away. Gandhi and Irish rebels made strange bedfellows.

Across the road from the jail, a shabby Georgian courthouse stood, with trees around the doorway and gardaí lounging beneath them. They showed me the entrance to the jail, which adjoined the rear of Kilmainham Courthouse (still in use) so that convicted prisoners in the old days wouldn't have so far to go. The great stone wall curved around towers in Norman fashion, though in fact the prison was built at the end of the eighteenth century. A dark entrance to the prison, like

Kilmainham Jail

a cave or an aquarium forecourt, was deeply set in the thick whitewashed stone wall.

Abandoned as a hateful symbol of British rule, the prison was later restored by an eager group of enthusiasts, hard-pressed for funds. With the passing years, Kilmainham became seen as a place of proud martyrdom. In England, only steam railways are restored in this manner. Unlike apolitical railway enthusiasts, the Friends of Kilmainham could be expected to have Irish nationalist sympathies.

I was told to go through to the main hall and wait for a guide. A passage between great grim stone-slabbed walls led into a large prison hall, ringed by two balcony landings. Zig-zags of iron staircases, at each end of the hall, led from landing to landing. Doors lined the walls at short intervals, on the ground floor where I stood, and around the landings. In other words, Kilmainham was built on the same plan as most nineteenth-century prisons still in use in England. Bereft of prisoners, who can be cheerful chaffing souls, it seemed a place of grey and derelict horror. Rows of glass cases, containing rebel memorabilia, filled a floor space once occupied by tables and chairs and used for "free association" or "break."

Big tense men, with bull necks, staring eyes and harsh accents, presided over a table of guide books and souvenirs. Two family parties, some foreign students and two shock-headed young men with film cameras made up the rest of the public. As the guide seemed a long time coming, we began to drift from case to case. Here many bold men, who spat in the eye of authority, had awaited death by rope or bullet. Some had been reprieved, some had escaped over the walls and some had served their term and left quietly. Beginning as a model prison for general wrongdoers in 1787, Kilmainham had, by 1909, evolved into a jail reserved for political prisoners.

Musingly, I read various incitements to rebellion. "Pay no rent...no rent...no rent! The Creator made the world as a gift for everyone." One revolutionary handbill had been "Issued by Ghosts." What ghosts must now walk in Kilmainham at night! Pictures of prominent rebels gave me some idea of what the spectres might be like. There was Dan Breen and his gang, all resembling brash, cocky, Chicago gangsters. Kevin Barry, who died in Mountjoy Prison, appeared as a guest ghost in a drawing that showed an actorish face, the dark film-star hair smarmed down. Michael Collins seemed a nasty piece of work—the notes said that "he had shot five informers in their beds." My favourite prison portrait was that of jolly old sidewhiskered Skin the Goat. He had been the cabbie or "jarvey" who had given the Invincibles a ride through Phoenix Park on the fateful day in 1882 when this secret society set out to kill the English Chief Secretary and the Under-Secretary, as they too rode through the park. Both secretaries were killed, but most of the Invincibles were caught, and Skin the Goat along with them. Kilmainham received them with open iron doors.

Political prisoners had been allowed to wear their own clothes. One prison picture showed a comic scene of rebels lounging imperiously at tables in the great hall. All wore shiny top hats like capitalists in a *Daily Worker* cartoon. Of course, many of the architects of Irish Independence have come from the Ascendancy.

Also on show at Kilmainham was an iron triangle, beaten in place of a bell. Such a triangle has been immortalised in song by Brendan Behan at Kevin Barry's prison, Mountjoy.

Only one cell was open for public inspection—that of a Mrs Plunkett, who had transformed her dark hermitage by painting a small, touching mural of the Virgin and by hanging up a tapestry she had made. Both men and women were imprisoned at Kilmainham. Artistic Mrs Plunkett entered Kilmainham as Grace Gifford, and married Joseph, son of Count Plunkett, in the prison chapel. A few hours later her husband was executed. He had been involved in the 1916 seizure of the General Post Office under Pádraig Pearse.

Pearse, a barrister and teacher, had declared: "It will take the blood of the sons of Ireland to redeem Ireland." According to the guide book, "he was shot in Kilmainham on 3 May 1916." Kilmainham is unusual in that prisoners from two historic uprisings, 1798 and 1916, were imprisoned and executed here. In its model prison beginnings, a strict "no-talking" rule had been imposed at Kilmainham as at Pentonville in London. This had been seen, in both prisons, as an enlightened and progressive move.

When at last the guide appeared, he pointed out the dark, windowless "reflectory," where those convicted of talking were sent to do penance and reflect on their misdeeds. Later it became known, more accurately, as the punishment cell.

We stood in a narrow passage in the oldest wing of the prison and looked at unrestored eighteenth-century cells, with doors that opened outwards. Everything here was rusty, broken, unhinged, leaking and weed-covered. I pitied the volunteers who were to restore it. Their work had begun, lumberjack-fashion, in the prison yard, where a forest and dense undergrowth had been cleared in 1960.

Kilmainham's Catholic chapel had been restored to its former grey stone, grey-painted condition, with rows of benches and a high mosque gallery for women prisoners.

The tour of Kilmainham ended in the prison yard, below strong walls. A small cavity in the wall marked the place where the gallows beam had been fixed, with the "drop" below. Beneath our feet, the bones of the Invincibles continued to moulder. In a narrow cul-de-sac, the GPO rebels had been shot one by one. High above me, the rows of small semi-arched barred windows looked down, just as the windows of Pentonville Prison look across to the railway bridge at London's Caledonian Road Station. Closer at hand, under a makeshift roof, stood the German boat, once filled with guns, that had set sail for Ireland in those troubled times.

Pádraig Pearse, it is said, contemplated a German king for Ireland if Germany won the Great War. Presumably a German princeling would have begun Ireland's "Hanover dynasty," which would eventually have taken root and become a true Irish monarchy. Blood may or may not have redeemed Ireland, but this romantic idea, to my mind, somewhat redeems the grim figure of Pádraig Pearse, architect of modern Ireland.

Smiling, the guide showed us the Kilmainham exit and bade us a courteous farewell. I tottered from the house of death, and tried to remember the appropriate ballad:

> When Carey told on Skin the Goat, O'Donnell
> caught him on the boat.
> He wished he'd never been afloat, the filthy skite.
> It wasn't very sensible to tell on the Invincibles,
> They stood up for their principles, day and night,
> And they all went up to Monto...

and

> Then the clargy came in with his book,
> He spoke him so smooth and so civil;
> Larry pitched him a Kilmainham look,
> And pitched his big wig to the divil.

"An eye for an eye and a tooth for a tooth," seemed to have been the grim motto of Kilmainham.

I walked back to O'Brien's Hotel, first beside railway lines to Heuston Station, and then along Victoria Quay by the River Liffey, where traffic growled and fumed nose-to-tail and the embankment path was narrow. Redbrick shops and terraces, some in half-use, some boarded up, stood among grey older ruins. After a while, Dublin began to look slightly more prosperous. Citizens seemed brisker. Small houses gave way to gigantic churches and even larger Corporation estates, sprawling up a hillside. Suddenly I noticed a strange tower looming over the rooftops. A broken shape, faintly reminiscent of a Moslem crescent, stood spiked on the point of an emerald green onion dome. The dome itself rested on what looked like a black windmill, with extended ropes and pulleys instead of sails.

Full of curiosity, I made my way around Corporation blocks that stood at odd angles to each other, and cut across courtyards full of dogs and playing children. One block of flats looked as if it had been luxurious when it was built in the Fifties. Now the gardens were overgrown, and an elaborate fountain sprouted grass instead of spouting water. Most of the blocks seemed to date from the 1930s. Judging by the happy playfulness of the children, this was not a bad place in which to live. Some of the dogs that ran quickly by seemed to be truly wild. An excitable family of Alsatian puppies was gobbling up bread thrown out for birds. One square was filled with spidery criss-cross washing lines and roundabout-style washing poles, all hung with garments.

At length, by ducking beneath flapping sheets and hurrying through archways, I reached the courtyard where the strange tower stood, high on a bank. It was protected by a black wall hung with barbed wire, yet two modern blocks of flats leaned over the wall to gain a better view.

I shouted up to a housewife who was resting on the walkway wall, enjoying a cigarette, and asked her about the tower.

"Hey, Mary, what's that tower for?" she bawled cheerfully to a neighbour leaning over the parapet on the block of flats next door.

"It's the Guinness Tower!" Mary shouted back. "If you want to find out any more, ask the Guinness people."

So, retracing my steps, I eventually found Guinness's Brewery, in a smart street running parallel to the river. It was a beautiful Georgian town within Dublin, a grandiose barracks of the Hops and Malt regiment, with a barrier and a gatehouse by the driveway. An archway entrance was crowned by a lady's head. Nearby, outside a cottage named "Dwelling House," the porter's young family enjoyed the evening sunshine. On weekdays, the historic brewery was open to the public.

"That's St Patrick's Tower," the porter explained, pointing across the road to the sturdy windmill minaret. "It's over a hundred years old, with several floors for drying grain, but it's now disused altogether."

Satisfied, I made my way back to the Liffey, where crowds returning from the hurling match were exchanging noisy banter.

"Galway won! Just like last year!" a fan shouted jubilantly.

A dancing, singing group of Galway supporters jigged by, led by an uproarious accordion player.

"I thought it would be Galway," one old lady told another, standing outside a church.

For a moment, old Dublin of fusty snug-bar romance seemed to return. I looked up and saw, facing the river, that monument to old Dublin itself, the Clarence Hotel.

Within moments I was inside the parquet-floored hallway, savouring the grandiose YMCA atmosphere. If the O'Brien is ever full, I shall certainly stay at the Clarence when next I visit Dublin. The brown mulligatawny atmosphere was enhanced by the heavily varnished panelled walls. Wiseacre-harsh Dublin talk crackled at the bar, where nicotine-stained housewives pretended outrage at the jokes of a man in a wheelchair. A silver-haired waiter-barman dispensed jokes along with drinks and ham sandwiches. Dublin, with all its ugliness, could still be a delightful city.

Outside, the blue sky grew dark, but the luminous clouds did not. Fluffy-edged remnants of daylight, they seemed to be stuck on the dome of the heavens, slowly moving and glowing like strange yellow lanterns. To give an image of moonlit clouds, a day sky is often filmed through dark glass and appears a romantic night sky. Here, across the Liffey, a night sky seemed illuminated in false daylight. Eventually all Dublin became suffused in yellow, then in deepest blue.

An unkempt gang of boys swaggered noisily up Lower Gardiner Street, threatening to fight all comers. Bars filled with hurling fans. Feeling content with Dublin, I made my way past nymphs, vases, flock wallpaper, mirrors, mahogany and plywood to my bed in O'Brien's Hotel.

᪥᪥

8

BEAUTIFUL DUNGARVAN

Waterford, in County Waterford, is a port town on the River Suir. Here I waited for a few minutes outside the railway station for the bus to Dungarvan by the sea. Safely aboard, I was soon jolting past the raw, brown wild-looking Monavullagh Mountains. An hour or so later I dragged my bag from the bus at Dungarvan Harbour and looked about me.

A bottleneck street led into a large square surrounded by shops, the centre of Dungarvan. Coachloads of people, Irish, English and American, were all dragging suitcases into expensive Lawlor's Hotel near the bus stop. Painfully I dragged my bag through the square and up a narrow street that led to a big Catholic church on a hill, ever looking out for bed and breakfast signs. Two such signs sprouted from small terraced houses in a slightly seedy row that faced the immense church. At the second sign, I struck lucky, for the door was opened to me by a stocky, harassed woman of faintly Bohemian aspect, Mrs

Enright. She welcomed me in, and soon I was unpacking my red, white and blue bag in a ramshackle little bedroom, the small window of which looked out on an expanse of annexe-roof and then up towards a majestic mountain in the distance. I thought I would like to set foot on that mountain.

Pleasant domestic murmurings could be heard behind the scenes at Mrs Enright's bed and breakfast house in the morning, and soon the lady herself appeared to take my order for breakfast. She was accompanied by her twelve-year-old son, who acted as assistant. Mr Enright, a mild kindly-faced semi-invalid, made a brief appearance. I was the only guest, so choosing a comfortable chair from the great variety on offer, which included wooden three-legged stools, I made myself at home and looked around. Normally a row of shiny new encyclopaedias on a shelf is an infallible sign that nobody in the house reads. The Enrights were the exceptions to this rule, for Mrs E brought me in an old copy of the *Sunday Times*, as well as various Irish newspapers. "I read it each week— it takes me all week," she told me. "The newsagent gives me all his old papers. 'Tis good to know what's going on in the world."

In the *Irish Independent*, I read that people in Galway and Sligo, in the north-west of the Republic, had taken to seeing visions of the Virgin Mary on various occasions. Others, who hoped to see her, were standing on corners, doing their beads, and staring at the sky. The Catholic hierarchy condemned such behaviour as "superstitious." I am not superstitious, and having weighed the evidence, consider that some of the sightings may not have been of the Blessed Virgin at all, but of Celtic wood nymphs. A vision commonly reported is that of Our Lady sitting in a tree. Those of us who can see angels and visions of holiness are fortunate. If a priest cannot see anything, might not the mote be in his own eye?

Outside in the street, I looked in the window of Mrs Enright's newsagent and saw advertisements for package trips to Medjugorge in Yugoslavia "where Our Lady has appeared daily since 1981." Advice could also be sought from the "Seers of Medjugorge," who sounded like Yugoslavian druids. A painting of the Virgin as she appears at Medjugorge showed a frightening woman with the features of the goddess Kali. However, the Catholic Church in Ireland approves of Medjugorge, perhaps because it is far away and Irish pilgrims are not so likely to be laughed at by the English. Some Irishmen, like some Africans, are so afraid of seeming "backward" to Englishmen that they give up well-beloved customs, customs that are often admired in England.

Vast, gaunt St Mary's Church, the Catholic church of the parish, dominated the street. I crossed the road and entered the churchyard, admiring a garrulous sign that stated in bold letters:

No Dogs Allowed,
In Any Circumstances.
Leashed or Unleashed.
No Exceptions.

I don't blame people for taking their dogs to St Mary's churchyard for exercise, as the lawns and the cemetery resemble a windswept and macabre park. Behind the church, the cemetery led downhill to the sea in wide tomb-studded terraces. A stark stone wall at the foot of the hill prevented access to the seaside prom. Inside the church, a middle-aged lady looked as if she were warming herself at the candles around the feet of a plaster friar, an expression of blissful contentment on her face as she worshipped. At the altar, a happy, shabby old man contentedly placed candles into holders. The large figures of saints had faces that recalled those of pre-war Hollywood stars. I remembered an English friend, a housewife on a council estate, who had continually broken off from conversation and tea-pouring to kiss the miniature saints who sat around her. She would pick up a little saint and press it to her lips.

"You'll have to excuse me kissing the saints. You see, I'm a Catholic," she told me brightly. "My mother was Italian."

What a crime to try to take such a faith from the people! You might say that there is a certain silliness in some of the doctrine, but no church or system of belief is without its sillinesses. Secular doctrines are often all silliness with no God to redeem them.

I roamed the wide, melancholy churchyard and noted a pathetic inscription:

Of your Charity, Pray for the Soul of Catherine, the beloved wife of Quartermaster Sergeant Jeremiah Molony of the 55th Regiment of Foot. After accompanying him through the wars of China and India she departed this life on the First of January, Eighteen Fifty One, in the 20th Year of her Age.

I did my best, though praying for souls is not second nature to me, and then I recrossed the road to the land of the living. On the far side of Grattan Square, hub of Dungarvan, I joined the buzz of tourists in the foyer of Lawlor's Hotel. Most of the tourists were naive middle-aged American couples who believed everything they were told. This is the kind of tourist I like best, as they seldom wear shorts or carry knapsacks, and are always pleased when you speak to them. They were gathered around a slight bearded young man who was trying to enrol them into the Bible-Mulcahy School of Dancing.

"You will be instructed by my wife, Betty Bible-Mulcahy," he explained solemnly.

"That's an unusual name," I remarked.

"We added the 'Bible' to our name only recently," Mr Mulcahy told me. "It expresses our Christian faith. We dance and meditate at the same time. My wife has nineteen letters after her name."

Well, well. Near the place where I had descended from the bus, too encumbered by luggage to look around, I now found a large motor bridge that crossed the mouth of the River Colligan. Dungarvan was built around a natural harbour, the Colligan estuary. So instead of looking out to sea from this part of the prom, I looked across to another shore, dominated by the tower of St Augustine's Church.

Dungarvan was founded as a monastery by St Garvan,

back in the seventh century. In the thirteenth century, the wooden buildings were replaced by the firm stones of the Augustinian priory. It was these stones, and the thirteenth-century tower, that I was now gazing at from across the water. Part of the priory had been salvaged from the Dissolution of the Monasteries and had become a church. The long flat strand on which the church had been built was known as Abbeyside.

Before crossing over the Abbeyside, I strayed along the prom, hoping to gain a view of the open sea. The path to the sea wandered in and out of a grey semi-derelict factory area, where I was not at all surprised to see the broken walls and towers of a mediaeval castle standing among nettles in a boarded-off yard near a winding alley. Alleys, industrial squalor and bits of castle seem to go together in Ireland. The sense of wonder is not diminished by National Trust signs, car parks and picnic areas, as at English castles, but *increased* by allowing the castle to be discovered with the same amazement by each visitor in turn. This particular castle had been founded by King John in 1185. He came over from England especially to build it.

Just across the way from the castle, through open windows in the side of an archaic factory, I could see a great cylinder, almost the length of the building, turning round and round. Open hatches in the cylinder showed it to be packed with whitest salt! Men worked wheels that sent the salt flying around, and fiery light glowed amidst the saltiness of it all. Could this be a salt mill? Even more exciting, could it be the fabled mill that eternally pours salt into the ocean, resited in Dungarvan instead of on the sea bed, the salt millers employees of Neptune or of his Celtic deputy Mannanan Mac Lir? Alas, no. Enquiry showed it to be a tannery, the salt being used in the preservation of hides. Even so, the machinery looked antique. The back alleys of industrial Ireland may one day provide grimy treasures for collectors.

"There used to be 250 men here, but now there's only twenty-five," one tannery man told me.

Soon I reached the lower wall of St Mary's churchyard, far below my bed and breakfast house. Victorian St Mary's had been aligned with mediaeval St Augustine's on the opposite shore. The church tower across the water seemed to stand on the furthest tip of land, beyond which a view of the hills gave way to an open seascape. I returned to the bridge and crossed over to Abbeyside.

The walk to St Augustine's led me beside a sandy shore where sandpipers twittered and a young mother cheerfully guided her children on a crab-catching expedition with buckets. The church was now Catholic, but it appeared that in the recent past it had been Church of Ireland (Anglican). Modern Catholic glossiness had diminished the mediaeval atmosphere inside, though ruined walls and fragments of priory outside made my visit well worth while. A roofless deserted chapel at one end of the building could be entered only by climbing through a hole in a wall and jumping down on to masonry poking through brambles. Here I found a tomb belonging to an Ascendancy worthy, dated 1733, with a coat of arms and an inscription that said the man had kept a table for the poor. His own tomb, with its see-sawing flat lid, now resembled a wonky table itself.

Beyond the wide grassland kept sacred to the priory, whitewashed cottages in terraces made interesting exploring, and I paused for refreshment in a tiny dark bar with a friendly landlord. In the driveway of a modern primary school, the Blessed Virgin smiled at me prettily from a glass case.

🍎

Much later in the day, after a good rest, I set out to climb the mountain I had seen from my window. It was a very small mountain, and this suited me very well. Far from being an athlete, given to leaping death-defying chasms, I am cowardly and fat, and I intended only to walk up the flanks as far as I could before darkness set in. Green fields and black forestry plantations gave way, further up, to a red-brown bracken and heather wilderness. Above the bracken, boulders reached towards a sky of perfect blue. Heading towards this sky, I found myself swinging along the verge of a busy motor road. Looking back, I saw a farmer and two men open a gate, shoosh a large herd of Friesian cattle quickly across the road and into the narrow opening to a field on the other side. It was done very efficiently, and not a cow wavered.

Further on, I saw the landlord of the bar I had visited earlier, out walking by the roadside with two fine greyhounds, one white, one brindle. He called out a greeting, but looked alarmed when I crossed the road to talk to him. Rallying, he pointed out the lane, or boreen, that I should take to get up in the hills.

"These two are going in a race tomorrow," he added, patting the sleek greyhounds.

Still by the roadside, some yards further on, I saw a white cross with the date 1921 and writing in Irish. It was a memorial to someone shot on that spot at the time of the War of Independence. Soon, to my great relief, I was able to leave the main road and dive down a narrow tarmacadamed lane set between steep banks at the edge of the mountains. After continuing downwards for a while, the lane began to climb, curving its way uphill around hedgy corners. Stone walls, half-covered by earth, poked faces through the undergrowth.

No matter how high the lane climbed, with myself upon it, we could not leave civilisation behind. For every mile or so, around every seventh corner, there would be a bungalow set back from the hedge, with a field or two behind it. Irish civilisation is a cottage civilisation. Some of the pleasant bungalows might have been on the sites of former cottages and some of the inhabitants might have been living on the same spot as their forbears had done, although in a very different style. At O'Brien's Hotel in Dublin, the proprietor's brother once read me a passage from an old book about Ireland with incredulity, as the author had referred to the country people as "peasants." Nevertheless, in the very best sense of the word, the Irish *are* peasants still at heart, the bungalow the modern equivalent of the cottage.

Why else are bungalows built alone miles from anywhere, far up on mountainsides by the side of idyllic boreens? In England they are crammed together in suburban estates, each with a flowery garden. In Ireland there may well be a few flowers, but the pride and joy of the bungalow-owner is the field at the rear with the sheep, or cows, horses or donkeys.

The bungalow-owner is a smallholder. He may not make his living from the land, but he still wants the land to come home to. In times past, tiny scattered cottages would follow boreens off into the wilderness, and the people would walk or drive traps down to the market in town once or twice a week, stopping at every gateway for a chat. Now, when people drive down the hill in cars to town each working day, they may not always have time to stop at each bungalow for a yarn, but they know who lives in each place and they gossip as much as they can. Television soap operas might have replaced Celtic mythology, but the pattern is clearly the same. Even when tarmacadamed, the boreen drives straight to the soul of Ireland.

At one turning, I came across a tiny white cottage, with thick walls, a half-door and a thatched roof. Nearby, a small brown donkey grazed. On I went, passing a prosperous dairy farm. A road sidled off into the forestry plantations, but I kept on until the fields behind the bungalows met the dry red bracken of the mountain-top and the misshapen rocks towered to the clouds. Taking life, a brown clod of earth became a rabbit and scampered on its way. Eventually the boreen forked, and the prong I followed led into a strange cobbled farmyard directly below the ridged mountain-top. This remote place rang with shouts and merry laughter, as two teams of boys and girls in their teens played a noisy game of hurling across the cobbles.

I watched for a moment in astonishment. Behind the players, on the brown bare mountain, dark shadows of clouds glided over boulders and bracken. The game paused while a herd of cattle was driven across the farmyard.

Leaving cows and hurlers to their own devices, I retraced my steps to the forestry path. Ducking between the trees, I took a trail of the kind known to my friends on the Shropshire-Radnorshire border as a "tushing drive."

"Tushing logs," in that far-off land, means collecting the felled timber stacked up beside the path and taking it by wagon or lorry down the mountains to the town. Different words may be used in Ireland, but I know a tushing drive when I see one. It leads nowhere, as it ends in a wood where tree-fellers have worked, but if you are walking for pleasure it may suit you.

Although dusk was now setting in, it was still a beautiful evening, and across a brambly tree-felled hillside, I could see Dungarvan, the church tower and the sea. Birds sang in the high undergrowth, and swooped out to cling to delicate swaying branches. They were titmice, mostly great tits, and regarded me with heads on one side before swooping on their journey. Dark spruce woods closed in on me, bringing instant night. As I climbed, the wind poured over the mountain-top and set the trees aroar. I felt greatly relieved when the path ended beside heaps of softwood, and I could return once more to the open sky. Outside the woods, in bramble-land once more, I was relieved to find how light it still was. Before long, I was back on the boreen, walking rapidly downhill.

To my surprise, a rabbit jumped out into the lane and charged towards me. Suddenly it realised I was human, and veered away with flashing tail. Another rabbit appeared. I froze, and it lolloped slowly towards me, looking to right and left. When it was almost near enough to touch, it stood up, sniffed, and then hopped away in a leisurely manner. Hooded crows flew over emerald fields, the sea shone blue in the distance and the evening air smelled sweet.

In Dungarvan, taped fiddles squawked in Lawlor's Hotel, as Mr and Mrs Bible-Mulcahy put the dance pupils through their paces. I peeped inside and watched the middle-aged English and American couples self-consciously step-dancing. Mr Bible-Mulcahy dashed here and there on the floor's edge, meditating furiously and shouting out dance steps.

"My poor boy doesn't know any History or Geography at all," Mrs Enright told me over breakfast once she had shown her son off to school. "You see, at his school they're alternatives to Science, and he wants to take Science. Is the education in England any better than here?"

"About the same, I think."

"There's a tension here between the young English holidaymakers and the young French," she went on. "If I ever get any English, I keep them away from the arrogant French. When we were in France, people kept mistaking us for English, and wouldn't serve us. 'Ireland, Ireland,' we kept saying. A lot of German speakers in this country are really from Switzerland, and they're very nice."

In a narrow Victorian shopping street on the other side of the town square, I searched for John Eagan's sweet shop. At last I found it, next to an old-fashioned saddler's shop with a dark interior that smelled strongly of leather. "Eagan's Sweets" was a tiny slate-roofed shop with a crimson frame around the window. Some of the Eagan family had settled in a similar street in Cardiff, where they were neighbours of a Welsh friend of mine, a young welder named Errol. He had asked me to look up the Dungarvan Eagans, who often went to Cardiff on visits.

A little dark lady, Mrs Eagan gave a cry of joy when she heard that I knew her friend. Within minutes I was ensconced in an easy chair in the minute back room, a kettle boiling in the adjoining kitchen. Colm, a white "Westy" terrier, sniffed at me approvingly. Pictures of relatives hung from the walls. The son of the house, a dark-moustachioed rogue, was a disc jockey at a pirate radio station. One daughter was at college, another was an air hostess at Heathrow, married to an Indian.

"Don't worry about the shop; the door rings a bell

when anyone comes in," Mrs Eagan said, handing me a mug of tea and some cake. "John! Here's someone who knows Errol from Cardiff! My husband is well known for playing the accordion, you know."

Obviously a very good-natured man, John Eagan greeted me with a smile that never left his face. He was a short elderly man with spectacles.

"'Twas for twenty-four years I've had a sweet and fruit stall at the Hurling Ground and never missed a match," he said. "But now I've given it up, so it's just the shop and my accordion. I play at home for friends, although I'm always being pestered to play in the pubs. You can't beat the old tunes, the old songs."

"Well, talking of that," I said, "where's the Old Dungarvan Oak? I've heard the famous song of that name, and now I want to see the tree."

"That's not a local song!" he answered in surprise. "It's from up at Sligo. There's lots of Dungarvans in Ireland, so maybe there's one up there. It's a grand song, that one."

I asked about the saddler's shop next door, and John told me that it was one of the last in the country. "That's a dying craft. People are after coming to him from Cork and Wexford."

Mrs Eagan proudly showed me naïve paintings, out of perspective but full of vigour, that hung framed on the walls, between the family photographs. Mr Eagan was also an artist, it seemed, with a fondness for railway subjects. Contentedly, the musician sweet-seller puffed on his pipe and tried in vain to explain to me the difference between an accordion and a concertina. "Why don't you run upstairs and see my old accordion on the bed there?" he suggested.

I did so, peeping around the miniature house with unseemly curiosity. It was a red shiny accordion, looking much like any other to my untrained eyes. On the wall above it hung a photo of the Eagans on their wedding day, in the early Fifties. Other pictures showed their daughters at First Communion, looking to my Protestant self as if they had dressed up as brides for a game of weddings. Enchanting little First Communicants, usually aged about nine, are an agreeable feature of Irish life, walking to church hand-in-hand with their parents.

"There is a lovely place here, by the sea, called Ardmore Bay," Mr Eagan mentioned on my return.

"How do I get there? Is there a bus?"

"There's not, but I'll phone Tom Kiely for you, and he'll take you in his taxi. He lives only a couple of streets from here."

So it was that I found myself knocking at the door of a smart modernised cottage, one of a continuous terrace. Tom Kiely answered the door, holding a baby with a bottle in its mouth. His wife obviously had him well trained.

"This is little Erica. She's been crying," he explained. He dashed inside, left Erica with her mother, motioned to a car and we were off.

"I've been to New York," he told me, as we drove through golden countryside. It was a glorious day. "I stayed there working illegally on building sites for two years. Then I became a truck driver in New York State, but I came back when my father died and took over the taxi business."

Despite his time in America, Tom Kiely had such a strong local accent that I had to concentrate hard in order to understand what he was saying. In high, fluting tones, his words tumbled out of his mouth. Finally, he parked outside a garish amusement park, obviously closed. Tom was dismayed by this, and hoped that the trip hadn't been a waste of time.

"Don't worry, I'll amuse myself," I assured him. I had just seen a round tower on the horizon, and I was eager to have a closer look. Promising Tom that I'd telephone if I got stranded hitch-hiking back, I paid him and bade him farewell and galloped up the hill.

On the way, I paused to look at St Paul's Church (Anglican), a spiky Victorian building. Various Ascendancy types were buried in the churchyard. The principal Ascendancy family at Ardmore had been the Odells, who left Ireland after Independence, bequeathing the seaside prom to the people of Ardmore. Nothing could be less aristocratic than the present government of Ireland, which seems to resemble a fairly well-meaning town council.

Leaving the dust of the Anglo-Irish behind, I scrambled up to the round tower, which stood in a ruined monastery-cum-Catholic-graveyard on a raised embankment at the top of a hill. Open fields spread to the horizon, bounded on one side by an immensely thick, long stone wall. Perhaps this wall had once belonged to

The Ruined Cathedral and Round Tower at Ardmore, County
Waterford

the monastery, or to the long vanished castle of Ardmore. Part of it had been used to enclose a stud farm.

Following a twisty pathway of dust between the tombs and pieces of masonry, I reached the noble pointy-topped round tower. I could see the sky through the high window, as another window was placed behind it. Three rings of stone, like belts, seemed to hold the tower in place. Adjoining it was the sliced-off end wall of what had once been St Declan's Cathedral.

St Declan (sometimes called Deglain) was the holy founder of Ardmore town. The cathedral, built a century after the saint's death, had formed part of the monastery. Pieces of stone wall and archway poked from the long grass, uncared-for and tussocky. Fighting had taken place here during Cromwellian times, and monastery, cathedral and castle had been numbered among the casualties. However, the roofless cathedral boasted a neat gravel floor and a plaque giving information.

I love round towers, and I gazed up at this one, entranced by the house martins, little brothers of the swallow, who floated on the breeze in and out of the high windows, swarming like the gnats on which they fed. Nearer the ground, red admiral and peacock butterflies winged their way among the ruins and settled on ancient stonework to fan their wings in the sun. A little way away, standing on its own, with no official sign, was a stone hut of ancient appearance, in good repair, with roof intact and an open doorway. Inside, I saw a rough, plundered-looking grave. Only later did I learn that I may have been looking at the grave of St

Declan himself, in the oldest building of the monastery.

On the broken wall of the cathedral, strange little figures had been carved from the stone, Adam, Eve and the apple tree, and Solomon with a sword about to attempt the partition of the baby. The two would-be mothers stood by, their features rendered impassive by Time. To entertain them, a fourth party strummed a harp. I slowly walked up and down the ruined cathedral, trying to imagine it as once it had been. Defeated in this effort, I looked at the graves and, in a corner, discovered an Ogham stone, or Christianised standing stone. Notches had been cut into the side of the stone, as if to measure the passing of the arch-vandal, Time.

Huge graveslabs of eighteenth-century Catholics lined parts of the floor like flagstones. One of them read: "Here Lyeth the Body of Mr Thomas Fuge, d. 1711." More Fuges lay nearby. They ranged from honest Tom Fuge of 1791 to Kenneth Fuge who died in 1975, followed a year later by his wife Dorothy.

Tiring of the company of the dead, I returned to Perk's Amusement Park and the present-day main street of Ardmore. Two black dogs lay slumped on their sides, breathing heavily, in the baking and deserted street. Front doors of the terraced cottages were open to the pavement to let in the air. Some of the little houses had thatched roofs. One of them bore the name "Old Post Office." Thinking to buy some stamps, I went in, only to tiptoe out again at the sight of a man asleep in a leather-bound chair with a newspaper over his face. Obviously it was now a private house, over-decorated with pictures and furniture. Two querns, or small millstones, were propped against the wall outside. Querns are the earliest form of millstone, used before mills had been invented, when peasants ground their own corn by hand. Their use survived in Ireland until the nineteenth century, but they are now kept only as ornaments.

At the end of the street, I gave a cry of delight at the wonderful view of Ardmore Bay. Steps led down from the Odells' prom to the beach, where gulls wheeled over the blue sea. The bay curved round, and I could see green fields on the flanks of the hills on the opposite shore. A Gothic boathouse beside the prom had once been the home of the Ardmore lifeboat. Now it was a private dwelling, with a fine window where the launching door had been. Next to it stood the Catholic church.

Shark's fang reefs of rock pointed out to sea in a cove far below the prom, and a harbour jetty had been built alongside them. Fishermen's cottages faced the jetty, with lobster pots heaped here and there. A youth emerged from a cottage carrying a milk bottle; in moments he was down the steep stone cliff to the jetty. There, holding a rope tied to a ring in the wall, he swiftly lowered himself down iron rungs to the sea, where a small blue fishing-boat awaited him with four men on board. Still holding the milk, he jumped in and the boat chugged away over the azure sea. There's deftness for you!

In the Cliff House Hotel, overlooking the sea, I enjoyed a sumptuous tea. At the next table, a cheerful family party included a jolly-looking nun. After tea, I roamed entranced around the hotel gardens, which descended in wide terraces down the sides of the cliff. Low maze-style hedges enclosed soft green lawns with apple trees and ripe apples rolling in the grass. Elsewhere, hydrangeas and fuchsias blossomed.

Overcome by the beauty of it all, a wasp "went native" and sucked nectar from a fuchsia bloom, as wasps must have done in days gone by, before ice cream papers and human beings were known. Scarlet fuchsia hedges marked the cliffside garden boundary. Below this, where black wet seaweed clung to steep boulders and sparkled in the sun, fuchsia bushes with berry-like blooms grew almost to sea level. I sat on a bench for a while and admired the view.

From the hotel garden, a narrow path led between tall bracken and brambles around the side of the cliff. A signpost pointed along this path to "St Declan's Well."

I was filled with excitement. I had never even known that St Declan *had* a well! Hurrying along, I saw stonework ahead, and ran forward under an ancient archway and into St Declan's old hermitage, now a grove in a forest of cliffside bracken. Standing on its own among the bracken, the archway looked wonderfully romantic. Now only the outer walls of the cell remained, crumbled down to chest-height in most places, with well-mown grass on St Declan's Floor. Feeling light-hearted and almost light-headed in this holy spot, I touched the knobbly eighth-century cross that stood on a portion of wall, above a stoop for holy water. Stepping through a broken entrance, I walked on for a few steps and then turned.

I saw, inside the hermitage, near the archway, a cave-like opening with roughly carved figures above it. It was the well itself, which I had missed in my first rush through the archway. Two dark windows looked down at a trough of bubbling water which seeped out into a ditch. Druids had once worshipped at such springs, and the two men carved in stone recalled Irish pre-Christian art, with their moon Easter Island faces. One of them was Christ on the cross, the other possibly St Declan himself. Ivy grew around their feet, and on three neighbouring leaves of ivy a bee, a butterfly and a bluebottle enjoyed the sunshine. St Declan is said to have died in this hermitage or oratory, and to have been carried to his resting place in the monastery.

A Celtic cross in the centre of the hermitage was surmounted by a ring of stone. Immediately I formed the notion that anyone who gazed at the sky through this ring would see an angel. I looked through the ring, and at once a white cloud drifted obligingly by and formed itself into a highly convincing angel, with dainty head and feet and large pointed wings. But then I have the gift of seeing instant pictures, usually of animals, in cracks in a wall or stains on a table-cloth, whether I want to or not.

For a while I roamed the cliffside until the return of the milk bottle fishing-boat reminded me that I too ought to return to my lodgings before dark. The sun was still high in the sky, but hitch-hiking sometimes takes hours. With a farewell glance at the beach where children were playing, and another glance up to the monastery, where the round tower stood like a black obelisk on the skyline,

I walked resolutely out of town towards Dungarvan.

Purple-blue cornflowers nodded to me in the hedges, rabbits scampered across the fields and grey wagtails fluttered across the road. The first car I saw stopped immediately, and I hopped in beside the driver. He was going all the way to Dungarvan.

"There, isn't that a lovely view?" he asked, stopping for some minutes beside a vista of the brown Comeragh Mountains. Nearer at hand, smoke rose from burning stubble.

"I live up in those mountains," my deliverer continued. "Myself, I sell farm machinery, but my father was a ploughman. Remember how friendly plough horses used to be, nuzzling at you? You never see a plough horse now."

We continued on our way, through forestry plantations, and soon I was in Dungarvan. I dined in splendour at Lawlor's Hotel. Irish businessmen sat eating together, around small tables, their shirt-sleeves rolled up to the elbow, their heads down as they wolfed their food, all the while talking and joking spiritedly. Only young couples sat in silence, with nothing to say. When I had finished my meal, I ordered coffee with cream. Coffee with cream in Ireland means a large cup of black coffee with an even larger lump of whipped cream dropped on top of it. None of your namby-pamby puny cups with a tiny plastic container in the saucer, marked "cream" and containing watery milk. For that you must go to England.

Next morning, outside Lawlor's Hotel, busy porters carried suitcases from a row of coaches into the foyer. Three Americans, a grown-up daughter and her elderly parents, walked along the prom, staring around them in wonderment. Now that I have been to America, I realise that Americans in the Old World are in a state of constant bewilderment and don't know what they are looking at until told. Indians newly arrived in England feel the same, and frequently bump into lamp posts, unable to realise that the insanely dreamlike scenery they are walking through is real. Americans are not quite as helpless as that, and although this party did stop at the first pile of lobster pots they encountered, at least they knew the pots were real and didn't try to walk through them.

Briskly, I introduced myself and explained the functions of a lobster pot. The Americans seemed delighted with the information, and so I showed them the castle fragments by the tannery. Somehow, while I was trying to take them back to their hotel, we came across Dungarvan's Anglican church, which I had never seen before. A strange stone wall stood on its own in the graveyard, full of neat purpose-built round holes. This stumped all of us, and I asked a passing housewife if she knew why the holes were there. Greatly interested and excited, the woman gave a long speech, addressing herself to the Americans as if they were her oldest friends in the world.

"As children at school, we all said it had been the wall of a leper colony, and the holes was where they poked food through for the lepers that were there. There was a great shipwreck many years ago, and the victims were buried in a communal grave here in the Protestant churchyard. You can tell this church is Protestant now by the English names on the tombstones. What do you think of young people today? There's too many teenagers—piles and piles of teenagers! Very selfish, they are; they don't notice anyone else, never say hello or try to get to know people. I tell you, on my life, Irish friendliness will be gone when they are grown. They don't even think about work. Work is a thing of the past. Now, my husband's been out of work for three years. It's pathetic, he can't get a fag but he has to ask me. And why should I be after giving him cigarettes? I earn just over the limit, so the state won't give him any money at all. He's fifty-four, so it's impossible for him to find work. He says 'I'm a dead man.' You see, he worked for an engineering firm, and all the men went on strike for the sake of one man that was laid off with no redundancy pay. So then the firm closed down! They had been looking for any excuse to close..."

There was a great deal more of this, and it all pleased the Americans greatly. They kept breaking in with sympathetic remarks ("Oh, say now!") and grew more Irish as I watched them. Eventually, we moved on, and as soon as we approached Grattan Square, John Eagan the sweet shop man approached, full of bonhomie.

"Hello, I'm showing these visitors around the

historical sights of the town," I said.

"History, is it," he enquired with spirit. "I can tell you all a few things. Our castle was built by St John, and there was a great famine in Ireland in 1460 or 1640 or something."

This proved a little too Irish for the kind Americans, and they murmured excuses and made for their hotel. Mr Eagan asked me back for tea. Soon we were sitting in the rear of the sweet shop, the soul of comfort, while Mrs Eagan waited on us.

"Our taxes pay for all that," John Eagan remarked, as some royal extravaganza or other appeared on the television screen. He had forgotten about Independence, an easy thing to do in a town as historic as Dungarvan.

After a light snack, Mr Eagan went upstairs and fetched his accordion. He strapped it on and played a toe-tapping selection of hornpipes.

"Before the harbour silted up, we got plenty of boats here," he told me. "Once a coloured sailor from Trinidad heard me play the accordion, and got me to show him how. He ended up buying the accordion off me. I remember when I was a boy, sailing schooners would come up the river, tacking this way and that with the wind. Young people now don't know what it's like to see rows of sailing vessels of all kinds, and old sailors who had been around the Horn, sitting telling yarns, drinking and singing. They led very hard lives, those old sailors, and I learned many an old tune from them. Here's one called 'Londonderry Hornpipe'..."

My favourite of Mr Eagan's tunes was called "The

King of the Fairies." Halfway through I thought I recognised the chorus of a sea-shanty, "I'll Go No More a-Roving."

◆

It was my last morning for breakfast with Mrs Enright, for I had asked Tom Kiely to drive me to Cashel, in Tipperary's South Riding. I had been there before, and knew Cashel to be the holy city of Irish holy cities, as well as a seat of Irish royalty. The palaces on the Rock of Cashel are Ireland's ruined Taj Mahal.

"Do you think there should be an Irish king?" I asked Mrs Enright.

"Ireland could never afford a king," she said. The idea seemed to take hold of her, however, for when she returned with a cup of tea, she seemed seized by feverish excitement, and had to put her cup down before she spilled it. "We had kings and Christian teachers when you were living in caves—no, in holes in the earth!" she cried. "We civilised you—missionaries went out from Ireland. Our people made wonderful works of gold, we had wonderful craftsmen! If only we had kept our language, like the Welsh! Sometimes when I turn on the telly, I don't know if I'm in Ireland or in England!

"Do you know the reply Shane O'Neill gave to Queen Elizabeth I when she tried to make him an earl? 'What do I want with your earls, when I can be king in my own country?'

"Now all we can do is go to places like Cashel and

think of our past! Every year, St Declan would walk from his cell at Ardmore over the mountains to Cashel—think of that! And there he and other holy men would meet with the kings of Munster. I'll say no more—go and enjoy Cashel."

I went, considerably impressed by the passion and patriotism of Mrs Enright. Shane O'Neill, an Ulster chieftain who murdered his way to the throne and who spent much of his time pillaging rival territory, had been more than a match for Queen Elizabeth in her doomed plans to Anglicise Ireland. Where Queen Elizabeth failed, television has been partially successful.

The ancient (and modern) province of Munster included counties Waterford, Tipperary, Cork, Kerry, Limerick and Clare—the south-west of Ireland. Each province, in ancient times, contained several kingdoms. Now I had seen the hidden fires of Mrs Enright, I could well see how the lofty Ascendancy interest in Irish folklore had swiftly led to Independence and the Ascendancy's undoing.

At the corner of Grattan Square, two accordionists were playing, one old with a wild grey beard, the other young and friendly-looking. Passers-by stopped and threw them money. A skinny old woman began to dance, kicking up her knees and cackling with laughter as the reels reeled out. "It brings out the Irishness in me!" she cried.

I picked up my red, white and blue bag anew, and headed for Tom Kiely's house. Suddenly I heard a shout and it was Tom passing by chance in his red grocery van. He gave me a lift to his front door, where his young brother-in-law was waiting. Apparently the brother-in-law was to be my driver for the day. There was no bus service to Cashel. So I said goodbye to Mrs Martina Kiely and the children, and made off to Cashel in County Tipperary.

We took the road that led past the mountain, and I enquired about the cross at the wayside.

"That's for an old IRA man who was shot," came the reply. "It's just a memorial—he's not buried there."

With that, he drove on in silence, occasionally softly singing "My Old Dungarvan Home." Although he was a shallow film-star-like young man in appearance, I suspected that he had hidden depths. It soon turned out that he was mad on citizen's band radio, and he began talking to his sister, Mrs Kiely, over a microphone, using bizarre nicknames and saying "Breaker!" He even tried to talk to passing lorry drivers in this way, but they didn't answer.

After a while, he pointed out a white statue of a greyhound by the roadside. "That's Master McGrath, a champion greyhound. He died during a race, so his owners put up this statue. But the vandals smashed it up, so the State stepped in and restored it, and now it's a national monument."

Before long, we reached the strange town of Clonmel, with a lengthy main street and a wedding-cake church. Clonmel left behind, the ride grew more interesting as the brother-in-law sought short-cuts, criss-crossing through the boreens. A network of tiny lanes with overgrown banks and verges covered the countryside. Mrs Enright had told me that "een" on the end of a word signified "smallness," and some of those lanes were very small (or eeny weeny) indeed.

Harvest was over, stubble was burning in the fields and the grassy verges rustled with rats. Again and again we encountered big brown rats leaping nervously around. They seemed to be young animals that had not known a harvest before.

"See, when the stubble's burning, the rats lose their homes and run out bewildered, not knowing where to go," my driver said with pity in his voice. "Then again, there's big grey rats live among the sugar beet and they jump out when it's harvested."

Having taken pains to avoid the rats, the brother-in-law placed my bag and myself on a street corner in Cashel and drove rapidly away, shouting "Breaker One!" into his microphone.

9

ON FOTA ISLAND

One day, when swooping low over the Irish mountains, Satan paused to bite a chunk out of one of them, before flapping his batwinged way across the plains of Tipperary. Ever since that day, that mountain has been known as the Devil's Bit.

Not liking the taste of Irish stone, the Evil One spat out his mouthful onto the plains below. This great stone is now known as the Rock of Cashel, with a ruined castle, cathedral and round tower on the top, and a town around the base.

For this remarkable lesson in geology, I am indebted to one of my favourite writers, George Borrow. Better known for his writings on gypsies and his travels in Wales and Spain, Borrow included a few chapters on Ireland in his autobiographical semi-novel, *Lavengro*. In 1815, the schoolboy Borrow had travelled with his father's regiment to the plains just outside Cashel. There he learned a smattering of the Irish language, and much

The Rock of Cashel

folklore, from an Irish schoolfellow named Murtagh. Borrow's few Irish chapters are among the most vivid he has written.

In the town of Cashel, I stayed at Grant's Castle Hotel, converted from an old fortress tower. Could this have been the castle home of robber Jerry Grant, the outlaw who so plagued Borrow's regiment? A bold giant of a man, full of fight and good humour, Jerry was said to be in league with the people of peace (or fairies). He was able, apparently, to summon up a storm at will to confound his enemies. Suddenly confronting the youthful George Borrow, in the midst of a snowstorm, Jerry decided to kidnap the boy and take him to his ruined castle hideout. Borrow answered him bravely in Irish, no doubt with an English accent. This tickled Jerry so much that he allowed the youth to go in peace.

At Cashel's Folk Village, an open-air museum, I read a late-Victorian diary in which the Irish writer expressed his ecstasy at discovering and learning to speak the Irish language. It was possessing the Irish language, revealed the diarist, that made him renounce Britain and take up the cause of Home Rule.

How quickly one generation's ecstasy is made the next generation's torment! When Ireland became independent, the Irish language was taught in schools, and became compulsory for civil service candidates and for university matriculation. Soon children were groaning almost as dismally as if Irish had been Latin. Sometimes it seems to me that nobody can enjoy an art form or philosophical idea without imposing it on the next generation of schoolchildren. Marxists have been the worst offenders in this respect, as they have imposed their ideas on whole nations. Perhaps I would have enjoyed English literature at school if there had been no exams, so that I could have read for pleasure. As it was, I secretly read Brendan Behan under my desk-lid.

Leaving Cashel, I journeyed westward to the city of Cork. Known as the Rebel City, Cork has very few public parks. So after admiring the fine shopping streets of the city, I sought natural beauty just outside it.

Here I was not disappointed. How wonderful to see Blarney Castle, the mediaeval ramparts rising abruptly from idyllic streams and flower gardens! Nearby, the stately home that had replaced the castle as an Ascendancy domain stood on a rise overlooking a park teeming with deer.

On the topmost tower of ruined Blarney Castle, a keeper swung tourist after tourist head-first over the rim of the battlements to kiss the Blarney Stone. If the stone should ever lose its power to grant eloquence, the keeper will be able to make a living as a Baptist minister. His grip and swing exactly resembled those of a pastor swooshing converts in and out of a baptismal tank. From the lawn below the castle, the stone-kissing looked particularly alarming. Only an iron bar protected me from certain death from a falling American tourist. The magic stone ought to be prised from the outer wall and placed at the bottom of the tower steps.

Another lovely park I discovered was the wildlife park at Fota Island. Nowadays the Irish are a nation of zookeepers. The English have lost the God-given capacity of caring for animals in captivity.

The creation of a parkland zoo at Fota Island, where animals could be seen "in natural surroundings," had struck a chord of delight on the harp-string of the Irish soul. Everywhere I went in Cork, I heard people asking if their friends had been to Fota Island yet. Love of children is one of the most admirable qualities of the modern Irish, and so is the love of an outing with children. I ran to Cork Station and jumped on a crowded train. Off we went to Fota Island!

First of all, on the flat wasteland outside the city, we saw the Gothic tower of Blackrock Castle, complete with flag. Industrial wastes led to mud wastes and sandbanks with sandpipers running up and down. A long bridge took us across the tidal mud surrounding wide Lough Mahon. A lough is a loch or lake. Wet reedland with wading birds gave way to tall trees and lush fields on solid ground, and the train halted at the tiny station of Fota Island.

Everybody crowded onto the platform, all talking at once, and we all got stuck in the tiny exit from the station, a relic of pre-zoo days. Impatiently I waited my turn, and soon found myself in a long dark avenue of trees, obviously leading towards a great house. Following the crowds, I turned aside from the driveway and entered another gate. For a small fee, I was admitted to the zoological park.

Inside, I found myself standing among seated groups of merry picnickers, with children running about everywhere. A café shed faced a large lawn with spreading trees, and a long lake with swans and ducks. Once upon a time this had been a corner of the Fota House park. When the Dublin Zoo people arrived a few years ago, they found the place as overgrown as the Sleeping Beauty's castle. They hacked away the undergrowth and restored the park they found underneath. Often they did not know what to expect: an avenue of palm trees had been uncovered beside the lake. No one had known of their existence, for the sub-tropical trees had been completely buried by the surrounding foliage. Yet they were still alive and I was able to walk beneath their fronds. They had been planted, it was later discovered, in 1880.

Stepping around the groups of happy families, I was amazed to see a furry shape bound by—a great grey kangaroo! It was not at large among the public, as I had first thought, but was living with its colony in a large paddock separated from the public by a moat.

Just as well, I thought to myself. The great grey, largest of kangaroos, will fight fiercely if cornered, and one can disembowel a man with its huge hind feet and kill a dog by holding it below water with its powerful forepaws. Or so I had read.

To my surprise, I noticed that a small group of children had climbed into the paddock for a game of hunt the kangaroo. All the grown-ups outside smiled indulgently. As the children approached, the roos sat bolt upright in the grass, black eyes staring in amazement. Their forepaws, armed with long spiky claws, dangled loosely. A pair of ears poked nervously from a mother roo's pouch slit. Then the whole party of giant roos bounded away.

Most of the human families at Fota shared this cavalier attitude to rules and regulations. At the cheetah enclosure, everyone who passed by climbed cheerfully over the protecting outer rail and a small boy twiddled his fingers through the wire at the indifferent hunting leopards.

Large islands, "planted" with dead trees and criss-cross branches, stretched in a line across the whole lake chain. Each artificial island swarmed with monkeys, or creatures of the monkey family, such as black siamang apes and cat-like loop-tailed lemurs.

These monkey islands must be a wonder of the world. Where thick woodland fringed the lake shore, it was easy to fancy oneself in a tropical jungle. A different species of monkey inhabited each island. Here were patas monkeys from Africa, ground-dwelling long-limbed animals that paced like dogs, red above and white below, with a fringe of hair growing outwards to shade their eyes. Big black wanderoo monkeys from India lived next door, with glossy black coats, fierce, disdainful eyes and silver-grey bouffant manes and tail-tufts. Some sat high on branches with their tail-plumes dangling.

My favourites were the capuchin monkeys from South America, which could hang from their tails or use their tails as an extra hand. When not in use as hands, these tails were curled downwards like a chow's tail in reverse, and used as an aid to balance. A little brown-and-black baby capuchin looked particularly comical as it stood on its hind legs by the water's edge and begged piteously, like a straight-backed little man with long arms and anxious rheumy eyes. Capuchin monkeys have black crests on their heads, which reminded their Spanish discoverers of friars of the Capuchin order. More familiar with monkeys than with monks, I was surprised, on a previous visit to Ireland, to see a house labelled "Capuchins." I hung around a while to see if they looked like monkeys. Finally a friar in a brown robe emerged, but his hairstyle didn't look very capuchin-like to me.

Had I been their discoverer, I would have called capuchins "teddy monkeys." The big truculent males looked like thick-set, vaguely threatening forty-year-old Teddy Boys, complete with black quiffs and sideboards sprouting from their reddish-brown heads.

Beyond the woods by the lake, I noticed a gate I had overlooked earlier, and so discovered the chief glory of Fota Island. This was the African savannah.

A wide sweep of grassland stretched uphill and down to where Fota House stood among trees in the middle distance. The large Georgian dwelling looked like a Welsh country house, gaunter and less luxurious than its English cousins. I walked among free-ranging herds of spotted axis deer from India and inquisitive rheas and guanacos from the windswept pampas of Patagonia. These are slim grey ostriches and wild orange-and-white long-necked llamas, respectively. A mound of stones at the verges of the path discouraged the animals from galloping too close to the visitors.

In the distance, I could see a line of giraffes on the

crest of the hill, apparently as free as in their native Africa. A little one ran on straggly legs to catch up with the others. Black-and-white herds of zebra stood here and there, occasionally setting off on a short stampede, then pausing to graze once more.

When I drew nearer, I found to my relief that a moat separated the African savannah from the public. Huge oryxes, large fawn-and-white hump-shouldered antelopes from Arabia, brandished sweeping curved horns that could kill a lion. I walked around the savannah and was on my way back on the far side when I noticed a brown dinosaur that twisted and curled its long neck around, keeping an eye on all who passed.

Closer inspection revealed the saurian to be a female ostrich sitting on a scooped-up heap of earth. A large white egg poked from beneath her dusty brown feathers.

"Look at that!" I said to a young boy who was passing.

With a cry, he rushed off and fetched his red-faced grandfather. The old man was much impressed.

"In the daytime the bird sits on the eggs, with her dust-coloured feathers as camouflage, and at night the cock bird sits on them, with his jet-black feathers," I explained.

"That's nature for you!" the grandfather shouted excitedly. "Who can beat it? Isn't that the most curious thing! Now when they try to bend nature, nature always strikes back."

An example of nature striking back occurred as I reached the lakeside once more. A boy of about nine, with a Birmingham accent, was nipped by a red ant, and began to *shriek*, to the astonishment of his Irish relatives. "That was a *red* ant!" he screamed angrily. "They're bloodsuckers! Now it'll suck out all my blood!"

Leaving the crowds of Fota Island Park, I walked alone up to the big house along a mile-long avenue. The few sightseers I encountered were holidaymakers from Germany. Virtually all the non-English-speakers I met in Ireland turned out to be Germans. Were the orderly law-abiding Germans attracted to a land more easygoing than their own, or did they believe the Irish to be enemies of England and therefore natural allies?

Irish easygoingness abounded at airy Fota House, where anyone could walk on the sumptuous carpets or sit on the elegant chairs, with no ropes or stern guides to restrain them. Little information was provided about the Smith-Barrys, the Ascendancy family that had once lived there. A gigantic spread of prehistoric Irish elk antlers hung over the stairs. Irish elk remains are occasionally found in peat bogs. No modern elk, or large deer, can match the size of those antlers.

The Smith-Barry family had obviously been fond of trees. Behind the house, beyond the peacock-haunted terraces, I walked through a dark, dank maze of carefully arranged mossy boulders overhung by great New Zealand palm-ferns. These were reminiscent of ferns and trees in pictures of the coal forests, long before the time of the dinosaur. Half palm-leaves, half giant fresh bracken, the slender fronds felt rough and grainy to my touch. On higher, more open ground, eucalyptus trees soared upwards, their soft bark peeling away from trunks of patches and tatters. Strange Martian plants overhung a monkey-free lake, but I grew nervous about missing my train and scampered back along the Fota driveway.

10

FROM IRELAND TO
WALES

For some Irish reason, Limerick Junction is not at Limerick but close to Tipperary town. In this part of Ireland, the countryside is very green, with many rivers and isolated square-keeped castles.

As I sat waiting on a bench at Limerick Junction, I remembered my visit to nearby Tip town fifteen years earlier. Tipperary town has to be so-called to distinguish it from Tipperary the county. A taxi driver had driven me to Tip town, exclaiming, "This is the dead soul of County Tipperary," as he set me down outside a squalid hotel. There I spent a few days, noting that sometimes my bed was made at seven o'clock in the evening and sometimes it was not made at all. For possible use in a horror story, I coined the phrase, "His face turned as white as a sheet at the beginning of the Irish tourist season." It can never now be used, for in the past decade the Irish have grown prissy and house-proud, their domains a mass of net curtains and place-mats.

Suddenly, while I was walking around Tip town, I had realised with a thrill that I was in that very Tipperary that the song says it's a long way to. Deliberately, I walked out of town so that I could walk *in* again singing "It's a long way to Tipperary." In those far-off May mornings, the Tipperary countryside was magically beautiful. Yellow irises bloomed all over the marshy fields, like giant reed-stemmed buttercups. Lanes with high banks wound purposelessly here and there, occasionally traversed by donkey-carts with milk churns. By one roadside, I found a memorial stone with the names of two or three men who had been "Murdered by British Crown Forces," and wondered if they had been shot by Black and Tans or executed by law. Sometimes I came across an old Celtic cross, worn smooth by weather and kissing, a figure still faintly discernible upon it. Country boys with peaceful faces greeted me politely. It would be a travesty to call these boys "teenagers," although Tip town sophisticates referred to them as "country jays."

"Boss, I'm tirsty," a big man announced in the seedy hotel bar. He then broke into a Republican song, caught sight of me and hastily apologised. "I used to work for an Englishman. His family had hunted the foxes with the same pack of hounds for three hundred years. Sometimes you'd see seventy hounds pouring over a bank! You'd never think the Major was a gentleman in his old clothes. We'd be better off under England, so, but our pride won't allow it," he added proudly.

Tip town in those days was a shabby unpainted place, with old houses of all shapes and sizes squashed together as if by a giant. Mangy stray dogs skulked in alleyways. A grime-covered stone fountain, water bubbling amid the rubbish, remained as a memorial to the landlord who had first brought running water to the town. Unpleasant-looking young men loafed around it. However, on my last day in the town, a funfair arrived, and all the young people cheered up amazingly. Boys and girls, sophistication forgotten, rode side by side on wooden carousel horses, to the sound of country and western music. Far into the night, the fun and excitement continued...but what was that? Here I was in 1988, and my train to Rosslare had arrived.

I found a window seat and watched Ireland flash by. We stopped at Tip town, then on past the Glen of Aherlow and the Galtee Mountains to Cahir, where a noble ruined castle stood beside the River Suir. At Carrick-on-Suir, Ormond Castle could be seen, with the Comeragh Mountains in the distance. Near Waterford, the Suir widened, and a succession of castles and abbeys guided the train on to Rosslare Harbour.

Here I found that I was *below* the town, which loomed high above me on top of tall cliffs that faced the sea. Everybody except myself seemed to be boarding the British ferry, for Rosslare is in the south-east of Ireland, the nearest point to Pembrokeshire in Wales. A steep road led to the clifftop and to rows of flashily expensive hotels with restaurant windows overlooking swimming pools and the sea. Down went the sun, 'mid molten gold and fire, but I was too anxious about accommodation to appreciate the view. At last, by paying for a double room, I was able to unpack my bag in a neat suburban bedroom. Rosslare Harbour seemed a new town of tourist hotels and suburban gardens.

My landlord was a young bearded Englishman from Enfield, with an Irish wife and several children.

"When I first came here, I was a barman at the Hotel Rosslare," he told me. "I've become a Catholic, but I'm not naturalised Irish. It would be an advantage if I were, as I'd get an Irish passport. On the Continent, they treat you like dirt with a British passport, but an Irish passport's respected. The Spanish are the worst when they see a British passport. They stop you at once, search you for ages and really scorn you. My Irish friends just walk through."

Marvelling at the continual changes in national characteristics, I sallied out to the Hotel Rosslare for my supper.

At breakfast in the kitchen next day I chatted with the landlord as he fussed over a sizzling frying pan. He told me that travellers begged from door to door in Rosslare, and enjoyed huge funerals complete with flower effigies of their belongings. Differences between Ireland's people of the roads and English Romany gypsies seemed to be evaporating. Effigies and fortune-telling used to be unknown to Catholic travellers. Some years ago, at an exceedingly tough gypsy camp in England, I met Nathan Lee, a scholar gypsy. He loaned me the manuscript of his still unpublished autobiography of rascality and horse-dealing, "The Luck of the Deal." In it, he not only mentions the traditional hostility between Romanies and

Irish travellers, but also describes a childhood visit to Ireland along with his tribe, who had formed an alliance with a family of travellers.

I had one day to spend in Rosslare, and that was a rainy one. A Kilburn friend had given me some photographs of his London family to give to his sister, who "lives in a lane outside Wexford. Anyone will tell you." He had not been in touch with her for several years. So, if only I could find the sister, I felt sure of a warm welcome.

According to the landlord, a mini-bus for shopping housewives would soon be leaving for Wexford, so I hurried to the end of the road to catch it. All the housewives looked disconcerted at my presence. By the time we were set down outside a Wexford supermarket, their hostility had increased, as passengers picked up by arrangement on the way, plus myself, had made the bus very crowded. I told the driver that I would be going back by train.

At the drizzly waterfront, I admired Wexford's natural harbour, a circular inroad of sea at the estuary of the River Slaney. A hived-off curve of shore had been bisected by the railway embankment and ringed by chains as if it were a town pond. An heroic statue and an old Customs House stood nearby.

This was Crescent Quay and the statue was of gallant Jack Barry. On the plinth, the inscription stated that gallant Jack was a Wexford man who rose to become Commander-in-Chief of the US Navy, appointed by George Washington in 1797. During the War of

Independence, he had been captain of the ship that forced the first British fighting vessel to surrender; an Irishman's revenge on England.

Turning up my collar, I hurried back inland and walked, dipping in and out of shops, along the narrow, twisty shopping street of Wexford, a street which crossed the whole town from end to end. Fairy lights hung across the road.

Entries between shops, with alleys and tunnels leading downhill to the shore, were said (on plaques) to mark the places where Vikings used to drag their ships. Vikings founded Wexford as a base in the ninth century, remaining until 1169, when the Normans had arrived under Fitzstephen. Not too perturbed, the Vikings moved on to Rosslare. A tourist-conscious town, thanks to its yearly opera festival, Wexford was covered in historical-information signs. What seemed to be a bomb site in the High Street was actually an archaeological dig. A Viking homestead was being excavated.

Halfway along the shopping street, at a crossroads, the seaward side of the road opened out into a square with yet another heroic statue, a green weathered figure of a rebel holding a pike in the air. The inscription was merely a date, 1798, yet that was enough. That fatal year saw Ireland's doomed attempt to emulate the American and French revolutions, and much blood was shed. Beyond the statue, a covered market led down towards the sea. It was the site of the old town shambles, and most of the shuttered-up market stalls belonged to butchers. The phrase "a regular shambles" harks back to times when heads, entrails and feet of beasts would be heaped about as cheap butchers' cast-offs. Scenes of gruesome murders are still sometimes called "a bloody shambles."

I stood on the site of one such scene. In 1649, Cromwellian troops took Wexford. First of all they knocked down a tall market cross that stood where now a green rebel of '98 roars speechless defiance. Secondly, they slaughtered three hundred citizens as they kneeled praying to the Blessed Virgin for deliverance. Thirdly, they sacked the town and left only four hundred people alive. No wonder the Catholics of Wexford replaced the sign of peace by a sign of war.

It seemed to me that small honour was earned by Wexford in 1798, for the town fell into the hands of a Mau-Mau-like gang, who tortured and killed Protestants under the banner "MWS" or "Murder Without Sin." Eventually, the Crown repossessed Wexford, and executed the Catholic rebels by the shore, where now a long modern bridge cuts across a corner of the harbour. Murder Without Sin must have been a delayed reaction to the Puritans' attack of 150 years earlier. The idea of murder without sin seems a Nonconformist notion gone mad, and was certainly held by the Cromwellians in Ireland.

English Protestants sowed the wind and reaped the whirlwind. The same attacks made by Reformation Protestants on the Church of Rome, attacks that led to the establishment of the Church of England, were later made on that same Church of England by a newer wave of yet more zealous Protestants, the Roundheads, Puritans or Parliament men. Similar ideas have reappeared in secular form in our day as the Doctrine of Perpetual Revolution. Institutions set up by a revolution grow strong, secure and smug, so that the same revolution must destroy its own creations again and again in perpetuity. Had I been a burgher of Wexford, I would perhaps have replaced the cross Cromwell destroyed, not by a fighting statue, but by a bigger and better cross.

Taking the bridge across the harbour, I looked back at windswept Wexford. Fishing-boats were out on the choppy waves, and there was a good view of the Customs House, statue and church spires beyond. Wexford is known as the Town of the Twin Churches, for identical pointy spires dominate each end of the town. Foundation-stones for both were laid in 1851, and the churches, fruits of Catholic Emancipation, were both designed in Gothic style by the same man, Pierce, a pupil of Pugin.

On the far strand, a bleak headland, I discovered a stone jetty that led out to sea past shingle, cast-up seaweed and rock pools. A sensitive young man, a German student, anxiously showed me a herring gull that crouched on the shore, looking at us warily but unable to fly away. I didn't see how I could help the bird, especially as I felt too nervous of its beak to pick it up. To cheer up the German, I pointed out the various healthy birds of the rock pools. Black stone wastelands were alive with small brown sandpipers who pecked about for food or raced along the sand flats. Tiny ring plovers with white faces and red legs scampered to and fro, while big black-and-white oystercatchers probed at mussels with long bills.

"I think those very small sandpipers are called little stints," I told the earnest German.

Back in town, the rain fell harder than ever, and drove me into one of the Twin Churches. This was the Church of the Assumption, in Bride Street. As I entered, I could feel the welcome heat of the candles. Faces looked up reverently at the figure of the Blessed Virgin. No service was going on, but the place was full of worshippers. Outside, just beside the wall, a name was written on the ground in large letters made of rows of white pebbles against a patterned background of darker stones: "Very Rev James Roche, 1858."

In a pause between downpours, I hastily inspected the other Twin (Immaculate Conception) and the Westgate Tower and city wall, a broken fragment dating from Norman times. Before Cromwell, Wexford must have been a beautiful city. Little now remained of nearby Selskar Abbey, smashed in 1649.

Back at the green statue, I noticed some incongruous shops. One was the Bridal Parlour and Hide Shop. It turned out that the word "Hide" referred to leather clothes, and had nothing to do with people hiding in bridal parlours or hiding from brides. The other shop, prominent on a corner, boasted a large sign: "The Cape-Bar, Undertaker, Groceries." A local landmark, this mishmash of businesses was featured on postcards of Wexford. I went in through the grocery shop, which sold fresh fruit, tins and sweets. Another door led into a dark old bar with curios on the wall. I had fully expected to see coffins on the bar with drinks resting on them, so I was rather disappointed. Apparently, the undertaking business was in another part of the building, round the corner. Elderly cloth-capped men sat staring at their drinks. The sweet shop lady did duty as barmaid, and carried my money through the door to the grocery till.

Determined to see all Wexford before setting out to seek my friend's sister, I roamed in the rain along a street of small, shabby, terraced houses. Suddenly I came across an enormous eighteenth-century-looking building, formed like a barrack square around a courtyard, with a huge front entrance. It had a semi-derelict appearance, but not quite, as if someone could be found inside somewhere. Was it a warehouse or was it a prison? A weathered sign merely read "WB Dunn."

An old man, standing in the open doorway of a terraced house, seemed to read my thoughts. "That's Dunn's, where they dry the barley for Guinness. You can go in and look around," he said.

The vast courtyard did not seem to be used for anything now. Perhaps in days gone by, wagons laden with barley had creaked into Dunn's behind teams of horses. Black open doorways and small glassless windows appeared stable-like around the yard. A cheerful man in a cap emerged from one of the doorways, and said, "I'm just going for a cup of tea—you look around as much as you like. That's the first crop of barley this year we're drying now."

I wished I could be dried like barley. In the darkness

of Dunn's, I found two forge or kiln-like rooms, almost caves, with open furnaces, like large bakers' ovens, roaring with flame. Drying machines, presumably full of barley, hummed monotonously. Huge wooden beams supported low ceilings in long empty rooms, for half of Dunn's had fallen into semi-ruin. In England it would have been made into a Barley Drying Museum, but I preferred it as it was.

Now somewhat less chilled, for I had forgotten to put on my oilskins that morning, I hurried to Wexford Station, by the shore, and asked a taxi driver if he had heard of my friend's sister.

"Indeed, I know the woman," he admitted, and drove out of town along a narrow country road.

Rain came down in sheets. I told the taxi driver to wait for a moment and ran up to the door of the sister's farm bungalow. Open umbrellas tumbled around the doorway showed that the family was at home. I prepared a tactful speech and took the photographs in my hand, as I didn't want the woman to think I came with bad news.

A stringy pinch-faced woman opened the door, where I stood like a drowned rat. With avid interest, she seized the pictures and examined each one with glad cries. Three young people, two girls and a boy, appeared behind her, wild as colts, with big brown eyes and freckles. They stared at me, eyes sparkling with excitement, but saying nothing.

"You're getting soaked to death—you'd better get back in the taxi," the sister said.

"Aren't you asking me in?"

"No, it's not convenient. Hurry, now, it's a wet day."

I galloped back to the waiting car, reflecting that the youngsters would surely have asked me in if they'd been in charge of the house.

No wonder my friend had neglected his sister for so long! She was a sister well worth neglecting. How lucky I was to have three friendly sisters at home in London! The taxi driver seemed a little ashamed at having been unable to provide me with an Ireland of the Welcomes.

However, there was a warm waiting room back at Wexford Station, with a friendly crowd, and before too long a train arrived. Like many ferry lines in England, the rails ran beside a street, past bar doorways, following the neat curve of Crescent Quay. The gull-loving young German was in the train, and talked solemnly of the "phenomenon of Hitler."

Before long I was within the warmth and glittering splendour of the Hotel Rosslare, and thawed out over a leisurely evening meal. Afterwards, in the Conservatory Ballroom, I watched pink young couples and small children perform wildly energetic dances to the slow lugubrious music of a country and western guitarist.

Next morning, I ran frantically for the ferry, getting lost and panicking, but eventually collapsing on board. With my feet on the seat in front of me, I fell asleep and did not wake up until the boat tied up at Fishguard Harbour in Wales.

How wonderful to be in dear, kind, friendly Fishguard once more! It is a town I know well, although it was a pleasant novelty to arrive by sea and to walk uphill into the town. At last I was among proper shops, selling the food I liked, currant buns and plums!

Friendly voices were all around me, in accents Welsh or English middle-class. In a trance of happiness, I went into a little shop and bought some Welsh cakes. "They have no Welsh cakes in Ireland," I told the cake-lady.

"Indeed *not,*" she replied. "You'll like these. I didn't make them, but my sister did."

Now that's what I call a sister!

Soon I was sitting in the sun at the edge of the cliffs, beside the absurd Gorsedd ring of Eisteddfod stones, looking down on the blue harbour and white cottages below, and eating Welsh cakes. I was among people I knew, for I was not only in Wales but in the Little England Beyond Wales, or Pembrokeshire. Thanks to Ireland's tragic history, many people there have layers of reserve and caution when it comes to dealing with the English. Others have old-fashioned deference and call you "sir." All such social uneasiness vanishes in Pembrokeshire, and I felt glad to be back.

Fishguard looked much the same as ever. There was the cannon among flowerbeds, and there was the pub where the might of a French revolutionary army had been locked in the cellar. (The French had better luck in Ireland, for a time.) By now, Irish families from the boat could be seen wandering around, perhaps in Wales only for the day. Husbands clutching bottles seemed rather tipsy, and wives kept exclaiming how cheap everything was. Children tagged along, looking around with big eyes.

In the dark little café room at the back of the sweet shop, the local Fishguard youth seemed under Irish influence, highly articulate, with the trace of a brogue.

"I've been around—around the locality," one eighteen-year-old boy boasted casually. Two girls gazed at him in admiration as he announced his plan of becoming a long-distance lorry driver as soon as he got his Heavy Vehicle Licence.

Quickly jumping into my own Heavy Vehicle, the local bus, I rode up hill and down dale, and stepped down at the head of a twisty lane. Swinging my bag and singing tunelessly, I traced the many twists and turns for a mile and then arrived, as so often before, at the little lost farm belonging to the Price family.

"You again, Porridge!" Mr Price laughed, taking his pipe out of his mouth. He is an ex-seaman with a grizzled beard and ships in bottles in nooks around the slate fireplace he has built with his enormous hands. A scholar, like his wife, his old house is full of books. Outside in the large stone-flagged yard, hens and ducks scratch and waddle. Kindly Mrs Price took my things and led me to my room with many a welcome.

"We were quite honoured that you wrote about us in your book, *Bizarre Britain*," Mrs Price told me over tea and more Welsh cakes. "But why did you say that the Chapel Sisterhood appoints the pastors? Oh dear! Was it to sell more copies?"

"Mrs Price, I was honestly mistaken. I never make things up on purpose, but I do make mistakes. I'm very sorry."

Mollified by my repentance, Mrs Price prepared an enormous meal, to which I did full justice. In order to escape from washing-up, I hurried out, put on the Price boy's boots and went for a walk in the woods.

These were magical woods, dark, with a green half-light rippled by reflections from the copper-coloured river in the rocky gorge. White spray buffeted across the river, and it was hard to tell which rocks were natural and which were part of the broken Roman wall. A wood pigeon flew noisily away on creaky arthritic wings as I entered the moss-hung abode of mystery. I made for the fiendish grinning druid face carved by a stranger upon the bole of a living beech tree in a lonely grove. Before the gaze of this tree spirit, I bent to remove my right boot and shake out a stone.

Huge dark wings beat around my head as I straightened up, and I fancied for a moment that I was being attacked by a raven for venturing too near its nest. Fanned by thrashing wings, I stood up and saw to my amazement a big blue-grey heron, its head and neck curled back in an "S" shape, flying away from me. At the druid tree, it straightened its wings and steered sideways around the tree like a clumsy blue woodcock. Then it vanished over the rocks and down onto the river.

Obviously, the heron, out of place in thick woodland, had thought my bent back was a stone and had tried to land on it. Fortunately it realised its mistake before perching on me, or I might have received a nasty peck in the confusion. As it was, I felt honoured to be chosen in this way by a heron, before the gaze of a magic tree. It seemed a good omen.

Back at the farm, I found that the Prices had sold their cattle, and now obtained their milk, free of charge, from a dairy farm on the other side of the lane. It was the dairy farmer's way of making amends for having built an enormous corrugated iron storage shed by the hedge, spoiling the view.

Feeling conspiratorial, I set out last thing at night along the lane with Mr Price. He lit the way ahead with his torch and carried a small churn. I carried a dipper-jug. Shining the torch about, my guide found the shed door, and soon we were inside a strange barnlike place full of huge metal tanks of milk. Uncovering one of the tanks, Mr P revealed a hidden ocean of milk, then filled his churn with the dipper. Closing the lid and the door after him, he led the way back to the farm. It seemed far more romantic than slipping out for cardboard milk at the Indian corner shop in London.

Early next morning, clutching sandwiches and waving goodbye, I left the Prices at Fishguard Station and took the train to London. Boat trains continually plied between Fishguard and Paddington, transporting Irishmen to and from London. How lovely the Welsh scenery looked!

After Swansea, the views became more bleak and industrial. Next came Cardiff, and then, near the English border, the dockland town of Newport. My mind sped faster than the train, back to the 1960s and the happy days I had spent in Newport.

In a large Irish pub, near the level crossing in Commercial Road, I had found a friendly *céilí* band, four big men of all ages playing accordions, fiddle and melodeon and singing Irish favourites and American songs by Hank Locklin. Hank was an American country and western singer who sang Irish songs in Nashville. There is an Irish village called Leighlin, pronounced "Locklin," so perhaps that was the home of his ancestors. This Hank Locklin-influenced *céilí* band was only the second *céilí* band I had then heard. The golden age of *céilí* bands was at its zenith, for Irish music had not yet been taken up by students or taught in schools as much as it is today. At eleven o'clock at night, the landlord locked the door of the pub and everyone went on singing, drinking and dancing until two in the morning. Sometimes the door rattled, a hoarse voice would cry "It's Fergus!" and the bolts would be drawn back as a regular customer slipped in.

At one point, the band split up to serenade three different bottle-laden tables, singing and playing anything on request. I stayed with the accordion players, fascinated by the younger one's Welsh girlfriend. The old, more skilful accordion player had silver hair and a kindly, wise face, weathered by a lifetime navvying by day and playing by night. His companion was fat-faced, with a cynical, shallow expression and a touch of devil-may-care. Somehow he had taught his girlfriend, whom he had known for only six weeks, to play the spoons. She played magically on spoons, the band's only percussion, and hurried the music on like an engine. Her eyes were a curious light grey, and were fixed on the musician.

"The band travels from town to town, and they're moving on in a fortnight," she told me. "I'm going away with them, to play spoons and take up a musical travelling life. My parents won't be too happy, mind, as I've never been away from home before."

I had my doubts of the wisdom of this plan, but it seemed romantic, rather like running away with the gypsies. What happened to the grey-eyed girl? Some years later, I stayed in a little country town on the Welsh border, and went to a café for my lunch. Irish cable-layers dominated the rickety tables, a reckless roving band, who had been working a few weeks earlier in Cornwall. They were all in debt at the boarding house, as "they don't pay you till the job's finished, like."

"I don't like those sort of men who work like mad one day and then have to take a day off to rest," one man said.

Another big man stretched himself, and announced, "Be Christ, I never known a town like this for lack of women. It's just eat and sleep and work. If it wasn't for me music, I'd go mad."

So saying, he took two spoons from the table and played a lively air. I studied his face, as I suddenly thought he might be the accordion player from Newport. If so, he looked healthier and leaner, but as all the men rose to leave, the moment for asking passed.

Musing on the Irish in Wales, I fell asleep on the

train from Fishguard, and awoke to look out on English fields.

11

1991: DUBLIN AND
BELFAST DIARY

In 1991, Dublin is the cultural city to be in, so here I am strolling down Baggot Street with its single line of misshapen trees to the place where the public gallows used to stand. Buskers perform outside the attractive shops of Grafton Street. One talented young man plays twangy plaintive notes with a saw and fiddlestick. Unfortunately, this fashionable prosperous part of Dublin, around St Stephen's Green, is plagued by roaming gangs of Mohawk punks and other exotic leather-jacketed hedgehog-heads. On this visit, I found the girl punks of Dublin to be most unhappy. One was sobbing bitterly, another swearing, while the young men staggered around jeering or hitting out at the air. Most of the normal Dubliners averted their eyes, so I did the same. I felt sorry for the punks—how terrible it is to be young!

Near Trinity College, I came across a most attractive newly cast statue of Molly Malone, seafood vendor and celebrated ghost. Bold, tragic and defiant, her proud features could be those of the Spirit of Ireland herself. In her wheelbarrow, sculpted cockles and mussels lay in sculpted baskets, looking very much alive, alive-o. Looking down at the pedestal, I noted the name of the sculptress, Jeanne Rynhart.

A beggar loudly sang in a doorway, and newspaper-sellers cried their wares, *"The Irish Times," "The Penal Times,"* and *"The Troubled Times."* (Some of these names may not be quite right.) I was handed a tract which described a vision of a golden-haired Mary, seen by a schoolboy. Edging my way through the crowded pavements, I headed for the place in Dublin where I feel most at home—O'Brien's Hotel in Lower Gardiner Street.

When I arrived, I found two wispy-thin yet round-faced boys assiduously polishing the brass door-fittings, including the great lion door-knocker. This unique hotel has been owned by the same family ever since it was founded, over seventy years ago. The house itself is Georgian. Furniture and many of the pictures and ornaments have remained unchanged since the hotel opened. A creaking mysterious place, where I put down my plastic bag and flinched from the sight of my reflection in the wardrobe mirror. (When I was a youth, friends assured me that my adolescent pimples would go away in time. Instead, all my hair has fallen out and the pimples have spread to the top of my head.)

Later, in the lounge, I met a jovial red-faced man whose home was a small village in West Limerick. We began to talk about Ireland's fascinating if disconcerting travelling people (travellers) whom I know fairly well from my own part of London.

"When I was young, the travellers used to beg from door to door. They don't do that any more," he said. "We still get the Wren Boys, of course. In most places in Ireland, Wren Boys are children, but where I live, it's adults who go out in fancy dress knocking at doors asking for money to bury the wren. At one time, they'd go out in the trees at night and shine a torch until they found a sleeping wren. Then they knocked it down with a stick. But now they just pretend they have a dead wren they want to bury. The Wren Boys go out every St Stephen's Day—that's Boxing Day to you."

St Stephen must be a popular saint in Ireland, with both a Day and a Green called after him.

John, one of the O'Brien family, took me into the quaint little office, a kind of porter's lodge in the corner of the entrance hall. There I admired old photographs on the walls.

"That's my father as a young man, the founder of the hotel," John told me, pointing to an earnest well-dressed figure standing by a table. "Yes, that's the same table as the one you see over there. In that photo, you can see Dublin's Nelson's Column, before it was blown up by nationalists some years ago. Instead of falling off his column, Nelson hung halfway down, so the army was called in to finish him off."

"And did they?"

"They did, and nearly finished off half Dublin too. Nelson was blown to bits, the General Post Office damaged and half the windows in the street blown out."

Both the polishing-boys stood respectfully to one side as I left the old hotel. "Yes, we are two brothers," one of them whispered, in answer to my query.

Passing another new statue, that of James Joyce, I trotted on my way to Philomena's Restaurant. Counting my money, I discovered that since my past visit, pound coins had come to Ireland. An Irish pound is now a dignified silver coin graced with the image of a royal stag. All the same, I wish the Irish would not copy England's customs, which grow sillier and sillier by the day.

❧

Near Dublin Zoo, I headed for Phoenix Park's gigantic obelisk, the Wellington memorial. From here, I descended a zigzag path to the main road below, near the River Liffey. This road leads to the village of Lucan, on the outskirts of Dublin.

"Yes, this is the Lucan bus," a slim waif-like girl with short reddish hair told me as a vehicle approached. "I'm going there myself, so I'll show you where to get down."

On the bus, my new friend chatted easily as if I had known her all my life. She used words like "Surely" as if Irish born and bred. Yet I soon learned that she had been born in England of an Irish family. Her life had been spent in England, Ireland and Wales.

"My father now has a smallholding in the hills of Wales, where he keeps both sheep and goats. He is a Gaelic speaker, and now speaks Welsh also. I worked for a long time in the Laura Ashley factory, but I missed Ireland and had to come home. Now all I need is a job. Here's Lucan!"

Leaving the Laura Ashley girl (who wore blue denim) at the local chip shop, I set off in search of Lucan's well-known ballad singer, Allan Scuffil. On my previous visit to Dublin, he had scrawled his home address on a torn piece of paper which I now held in my hand.

It was dark when I found the house. Allan's wife, Mary, a friendly soul, asked me inside in a whisper. A log fire burned, and grey-bearded Allan slept before it, on a sofa.

"He's very ill, so I shan't wake him," she said. "Let me warm you up something to eat. It's a very Irish supper, I'm afraid—potatoes, cabbage and corned beef."

Irish corned beef is served boiled and hot, not out of a tin. It tastes rather like tongue—a treat indeed. Allan soon woke up, and greeted me warmly. My eyes roved around the room, and for the first time I noticed that every shelf carried a bronze statuette. Some depicted children playing, others were of birds—an owl and a falcon, both feather-perfect.

"All these were done by my sister, Jeanne Rynhart," Allan told me proudly. "She's the one who made the Molly Malone statue in Dublin. Just look at that owl—what a work of art! Arabs come over to buy her bronze falcons."

We chatted on, in the cosy fireside atmosphere, until at last Allan felt well enough to sing a song. He sang "Four Green Fields," the lament of a "fine old woman" whose fourth green field has been stolen by strangers. Of course, the four fields are the four provinces of Ireland. The "proud old woman" is really Cathleen Ní Houlihan, the Spirit of Ireland, lamenting the loss of Ulster, her fourth field.

Most of Ulster may be ruled by the English, but it was originally settled by the Scots. Yet the Scots, we are told, originated in Ireland. So many strangers have spent their time trampling on Cathleen Ní Houlihan's fourth field that I hoped the good dame would not mind one more—myself. In the morning, I would be off to Belfast. Allan sang on, regardless.

🍎

A genial old cloth-capped man directed me to Dublin's "Great Northern" or Connolly Station. "That's what I still call it," he added. (Most of Dublin's landmarks have suffered various changes of name, along with the shot and shell of the 1920s.)

On the Belfast train, I sat opposite a fierce-looking man with a bushy black beard. We seemed to have nothing in common, and I decided he must be an engineer. Perhaps a good man to have about the place in an emergency. The day before, there had been a bomb scare on the line, and passengers had done part of the journey on a special bus.

Hardly had our train left Dublin than the man began to talk. "Are you going to Belfast on business?" he asked in a far from stern voice.

"Not at all, I'm going there to see the zoo," I replied.

"Ah, Belfast has a very good zoo. My wife and I used to go there when the children were smaller. I'm going up to take a course, as I'm studying to be a priest."

I nodded sagely at this, then stared out at estuary scenery. After a while, I reflected that I ought to tell him that possessing a wife and children would disqualify him from becoming a priest. Then, if he wished, he could get off at the next stop and return to Dublin.

"No, an Anglican priest," he explained, when I diffidently brought up the matter. "That will be a change in my family, as up to now most of the men have been army people. There is an eighteenth-century sword handed down in our family, with a French name on the blade. My grandfather was wounded in the Boer War, and always walked with a limp. A bullet ricocheted, smashed his ankle and he fell unconscious. When he awoke, it was night time. The battle was over and the dead lay all around. In the distance, he could hear voices, coming nearer and nearer. He didn't like this at all, my grandfather, as the Boers were supposed to kill wounded men. Just then, he heard a Scottish voice, so he yelled out and got rescued.

"We live just outside Belfast, in a house that my father bought very cheaply when he came out of the army. It turned out that it was a haunted house! We children had nightmares, and felt weights on our chests at night. Footsteps could be heard at all hours, yet no intruders could be found. Finally, my mother met an old lady who remembered when the house was built, and the true story came out.

"Apparently the chief builder had an accident while the house was going up. Somehow he cut off two of his fingers, then fell off the ladder. As he was carried away, he cursed the house, and so it was haunted as soon as it was built. No one could live in it. That's why its price fell and fell. When Mother heard that, she knew what to do. She bought lots of secondhand Bibles and placed them up and down the house, one under every pillow and one at the top and bottom of the stairs. We never moved them, and we had no more trouble with ghosts.

"I think a lot of ghosts are 'time warps.' A friend of mine once found an old-fashioned shop where an old-fashioned lady sold him pipe tobacco wrapped in brown paper. She stared at his clothes and money, but said nothing. He liked the tobacco, but when he went back, the street had vanished! It had been demolished years before! Another friend of mine dreamed he saw a horse rear up at a passing car, making the rider drop a small child he was holding. Ages later, my friend saw the same horse fall in real life, ran forward and caught the child as it fell..."

Outside the train window, I saw a road barricaded by corrugated iron, which formed a rough lean-to compound where soldiers could search cars and then wave them on. Beyond this stood a dug-out fortress made of sandbags. We had reached the Border. Unaffected by the change, our train sped on, accompanied by ghost stories.

"Look at those rabbits, and those old ruined cottages," I broke in.

"We have hares here too," my priestly friend remarked. "I once saw a mad hare run head-on into a tree. That was in March. Some of the old cottages are almost of prehistoric design. Young friends of mine stayed in a cottage for a holiday once. The farmer who owned the land put it all to rights for them. There was no fireplace or chimney, just a ring of stones in the middle of the floor and a hole in the roof over it. As for the stone walls, they were very thick, with niches cut six feet into them, at intervals, each niche opening near the stone hearth. That's where the beds were placed, and at one time a big family would have lived there all the year round."

I felt torn between two pleasures, as my companion's tales of old Ireland conflicted with my wish to look out the window. Backyards of small Protestant terraces faced the track at Portadown, some with large Union Jacks hanging from poles. Before we reached Belfast, the bearded man told me of an ancestor who had deserted from the army, then rejoined under a false name, an English surname.

"That's why we have an English family name," he continued. "One of my cousins traced our ancestry back to Scotland. We came over to Ulster hundreds of years ago, to Antrim, where we were known as the Black Ravens! So we must have been thieves, for a raven is a thieving bird, is it not?"

"No, I can save your reputation!" I put in. "A *jackdaw* steals, but a raven is a warrior's bird, a bird of death. Your ancestors must have been soldiers for longer than you thought! Perhaps they had black beards, like yours. When I was in the west of Ireland three years ago I met a family who lived near a mountain haunted by wicked Queen Maeve. They had a pet raven in a cage, a noble, friendly bird, who attracted wild ravens to the garden. It had been raised from a fledgling, fed on little strips of beef.

"This raven had been found by a farmer, tumbled out of its nest. He took it home to his tiny cottage, at the end of a long overgrown lane, and kept it in a box on one side of the fire. On the other side of the fire, there was another box, where he kept an injured lamb. One of its eyes had been pecked out by adult ravens. It was nice of the farmer not to have a grudge against ravens after that, as he reared both lamb and raven. If he hadn't sold the fledgling, the two creatures might have grown up to be friends."

"The raven shall lie down with the lamb," intoned the future priest, as we pulled into Belfast.

◆

Here I am, snug in a boarding house on Belfast's Sunset Strip, Botanic Avenue. One end of this celebrated avenue adjoins Queen's University and the Botanical Gardens, the other leads straight to the city centre. Sandy Row, famous for its Orangemen, is just around the corner.

Student territory, Botanic Avenue has a safe atmosphere, but has become terribly flashy. Expensive shops vie with Chinese restaurants and rows of neon-lit nightclubs for student gold. In the evenings, I have my late-night cup of tea in a replica of a 1950s' American milk bar, completely surrounded by sharply dressed unbookish students. It is now impossible to tell Town from Gown. Where are the scarves and duffel-coats of yesteryear? Where are the Causes?

I last knew Botanic Avenue in 1969, just before the Troubles broke out in August of that year. At that time, civil rights were all the rage, the students inspired by Martin Luther King. Posters of clenched fists and broken chains adorned many a bedsit window in Botanic Avenue. Central and municipal power in Northern Ireland was mainly in the hands of Protestants. These the student civil rights marchers compared with the "white supremacists" of the American South. Very many of the "fair play for Catholics" marchers from the university were themselves of Protestant background. Their cause was just, but the electricity it generated brought to life the sleeping monsters of Republican and Protestant fanaticism. No wonder the Belfast students of today shun causes and ideals, and concentrate on dancing and cocktails. Perhaps they feel that a secure "unjust society" is better than Terror.

All the same, it is hard to sleep when non-idealistic students, mostly young women, burst swearing and shouting from Botanic nightclubs at half past three in the morning. Each night, Town youths gather in a doorway outside my boarding house, and throw beercans into the road. However, such petty nuisances are as nothing beside the excitement of living on Botanic

Avenue, nerve-centre of the world. Last night I was awoken by the sound of Irish minstrelsy. Drawing the net curtains, I peeped out on two Belfast lassies tripping along the road, singing a Dublin song as they danced:

Here's a piece of advice I got
From an old fishmonger:
"If food is scarce and you see the hearse,
You know you've died of hunger."

Tonight, on leaving the milk bar, I caught a glimpse of the Other Belfast. Soldiers in battledress stood in the Avenue stopping cars and politely looking inside them. A sidestreet was taped off with long white strips of material, the makeshift barrier guarded by servicemen. Others seemed to be searching an hotel. Students and revellers walked around an army van parked in the middle of the pavement, eyes averted in studied unconcern. Two soldiers stood half-emerged from the van's open roof-flap, black guns at the ready. I never found out what it was all about.

Earlier on, I had enjoyed a pot of tea in a more sedate Botanic café, served by a waitress in traditional black-and-white maid's costume. Such neatly dressed nurse-like waitresses are a feature of Belfast. They can even be seen in the Linen Hall Library in the centre of the city, the only library I know that boasts a tea-and-bun shop. An old oak-panelled independent library, founded in 1788, it must be one of the wonders of Belfast. If you can imagine a cross between a Boot's

Booklovers' Library and the Bodleian at Oxford, that will be the Linen Hall. A grave club-porterlike man stands sentry in the doorway.

Soldiers turn up unexpectedly in the centre of Belfast, and I saw a group in earnest discussion near the Library, rifles pointing upwards. Compared to the visit I made nine years ago, the city seems relatively calm, though rundown in places. "Checkpoint Charlie" posts that once were manned by soldiers now have policemen on duty. Of course, the police here are armed. There is now a bright mural entrance to the Falls Road, and the worst of the flats there have been pulled down.

Back in Botanic Avenue, I walked up to the university, where once I had gatecrashed a huge strawberry feast, an annual event. On this occasion, I noticed that nearly all the students were streaming into the Social Science building. In my idealistic youth, I had been upset to find that false sciences, such as Social (or sociology), were being taught to impressionable young people at universities. Older and crustier, I now feel that any branch of human knowledge, however worthwhile, turns into nonsense by being taught at a university. Of course, I'm all in favour of eating strawberries.

🍎

Every July Belfast's Orange Parade sets out from halls in and around the formerly picturesque district of Sandy Row. When I first knew Sandy Row, in the '60s, it was still a place of neat terraced houses with scrubbed doorsteps and highly ornamented ground-floor windows. Dramatic paintings of King Billy crossing the Boyne ornamented the terrace ends. As you might expect, all these have been pulled down, and replaced by anonymous council houses. A shabby row of shops remains, along with several pubs and social clubs. The other day, I strolled up from my "safe house" on Botanic Avenue and had another look at Sandy Row.

Old-style Row houses, some boarded up, survived only in one pathetic cul-de-sac, Malone Place. There, to my delight, I saw a maidenhair fern reposing 'mid net curtains, a symbol of the Row I used to know. A Union Jack flew bravely from the roof of the Sandy Row Rangers Supporters' Club. Here football meshes curiously with politics and religion. Thick wire net on the windows of the Club concealed the interior. A door opened as I passed, and a cheerful old man stepped out with a walking frame.

Young mothers wheeled pushchairs in and out of the shops, and the pavements were crowded. Nearly everyone looked inoffensive and kindly. Family parties strolled in and out of dark pubs, fathers clutching toddlers. Torn notices on the walls, left over from the Orange parade, warned marchers not to "provoke escalating violence by jeering at rival loyalist associations."

Nearby, I discovered a vivid life-size wall painting, showing a seventeenth-century soldier and a modern British soldier saluting one another from opposite shores of the River Boyne. A white horse pranced across the

Boyne itself, hooves barely skimming the water. On its back rode triumphant King Billy.

Across the road, the murals were more crude. A cartoon bulldog snarled from the middle of the Union Jack, beside the Red Hand emblem of Ulster. Not far away, I saw a stencilled Red Hand on a wall, ready to be filled in later. Mild Methodist-like families, with children, stepped from their cars into the old red-brick Orange lodge. One car was attached to a small horsebox. Presumably this had once contained the goat, ready saddled for an initiation. What does the ballad say?

On a goat! On a goat!
To join in the Order you ride on a goat!

The Penal Times of the seventeenth and eighteenth centuries are a sad episode in Ireland's history. Anglicanism was the only permitted form of Christianity, and Catholics suffered accordingly. It was Christopher Howse, Catholic adviser to *The Spectator*, who first told me that Northern Irish Presbyterians also suffered persecution during the Penal Times.

When religious tolerance finally came to Ireland in the early nineteenth century, the Sandy-Row type Protestants must have been overjoyed at being accepted by the Crown at last. Perhaps their touching loyalty to the United Kingdom began at that time. Far across the sea in the British West Indies, former slaves believed that Queen Victoria had been personally responsible for setting them free. They too became wildly patriotic and this patriotism began to evaporate only when their descendants arrived at English ports. Some hold it yet.

A happier tale of persecution averted comes from the days of sixteenth-century Mary Tudor. As Catholic ruler of England, Mary gave Dr Henry Cole, Dean of St Paul's, a royal warrant to go to Northern Ireland and arrest Protestants. On his way to Ireland, in 1553, the zealous dean stayed the night at the Blue Posts Inn, Chester. There he met the mayor of Chester. After a drink or two, the dean produced the leather box he used as a briefcase. "I have within this box that which will lash the heretics of Ireland!" he declared.

He was overheard by the Irish Protestant landlady, who feared for her family "across the water." While pretending to serve drinks, she quickly stole the box, threw out the warrant and put a pack of cards in its place, knave of clubs upwards. She then returned the box. Next morning the dean set sail.

Safely in Ireland, the dean handed his box to Lord Deputy Fitzwalter and declared himself ready to begin the persecution. But when the box was opened, no warrant could be seen, only cards!

"There's no help for it, you must go back to England and get another document," said the Lord Deputy. "Meanwhile, shuffle the cards and let us have a game."

What with tides and bad weather, Elizabeth I was on the throne before the dean could get another warrant. It was the Catholic turn to be persecuted, and the Protestants were spared. As for the quick-witted landlady of the Blue Posts, grateful Queen Elizabeth gave her an allowance of forty pounds a year.

❦

On a drizzly, misty March day, I went to the Belfast Zoo. This zoo is situated on a hillside far out of town, with splendid views in fine weather. At one time, the zoo marked the turning-round point of the Belfast trams. A pleasure garden grew up at this significant spot, with a lake, golf-course, floral hall and zoo. When I last visited the zoo in the '60s, it was a national disgrace. The bears were still pacing dark 1930s' dens, ten paces, a swing of the head, and ten paces back again. Their faces wore grooves from rubbing against the bars.

Now all is changed. No expense has been spared, and a new park-like zoo has swallowed up the whole of the pleasure grounds and climbed high into the hills. Visitors are few and far between, at least in rainy weather, and the amazed ticket-girl, summoned by an astonished keeper, asked, "Are you really going in?" Once inside, I felt sorry for the two young couples I saw with pushchairs, as the paths from cage to spacious cage were very steep. Perhaps Belfast Zoo ought to emulate the zoo at Dudley, and provide a chair lift.

Still, it was romantic there in the mist, the lion's booming roar echoing from a sinister looming hilltop wood. I tried to imagine the reaction of Celtic barbarians of ancient times, if they had heard such a menacing sound at the dark forest edge. On a damp open hillside, brown deerlike animals stood half-hidden in wreaths of

white vapour. With a shock equal to that of a misplaced barbarian, I realised that they were not deer but timid long-necked guanacos, or wild llamas. Again the lion roared, the sound reminding me of a steam train on a mountain railway in Wales.

At the top of the hill, rare Peruvian spectacled bears ambled slowly through wet meadow grass. Thanks to the "no feeding" rule, the bears ignored the toddlers who had been pushed so painfully up to see them. Back at the lake, near the entrance, I admired the stately home of the spider monkeys. As I watched, a tribe of large black monkeys walked in single file from the house across a log drawbridge to an island in the lake. Near the island, their tails went up and hooked onto a horizontal rope, rather like trolley buses on a wire. All the monkeys but one trolley bussed up into the trees and began swinging among the branches. One monkey, however, made for a log lying in the grass and used it as a gym horse, performing rapid backward somersaults and handstands. It was better than a circus. Rain fell once more, and the monkeys hurried into their tall house to perform similar antics on a tree that stood indoors.

In the children's zoo, I explored a complete farm, with rare breeds of pigs and cattle. Here I saw a dark brown goat with white hindquarters, labelled Old Irish Goat. Some miles out of Belfast, I had seen similar goats at a farm near Dundrum.

Gentoo penguins from the Antarctic had a wonderful home in Belfast, a waddling ground of tussocky grass and a clear blue pool with a raised window on one side.

Through this I could watch the streamlined birds gliding underwater. Air bubbles flew from the crevices in their smooth plumage, as if the birds had been punctured. Some indeed shot forward as if jet-propelled, a stream of bubbles pouring out of their back feathers.

Cartoonists continually and mistakenly draw penguins in scenes of the North Pole, instead of in the South Pole. Until the nineteenth century, a flightless black-and-white bird, the great auk, lived in the Arctic. It was often called a penguin. Since the great auk has long been extinct, the cartoonists are simply working from folk memory.

Polar bears, cartoon companions of penguins, enjoyed the freedom to roam a vast rocky enclosure at Belfast Zoo. A waterfall plunged twenty feet into a turbulent pool. All the same, I couldn't help wishing that the bears had been given some tussocky grass and earth beneath their feet, as had the penguins. Wild polar bears often roam inshore on the tussocky tundra, and need a change from rocks and ice. Why not let them try the advantages of a southern climate, with grass, bushes and trees?

One polar bear, I noticed, did not frolic with the rest. He had found a flat piece of land and paced it monotonously: ten paces, a swing of the head, turn and ten paces more. I thought I recognised this bear as a veteran of the bad old days in Belfast.

￼

I journeyed back to Dublin on a train full of excited

would-be revellers. For the date was 17 March, St Patrick's Day, and Dublin was holding a grand parade.

Running from the station, I hurried to O'Connell Street. A huge green crane, with cameramen aloft, loomed over the crowds of spectators. Wild children, vendors of every kind, and gardaí with megaphones surged over the pavements. In the road, platoons of scouts, guides and brownies were marching along.

Huge ornate floats came next, full of make-believe Edwardians and Victorians. Plenty of cyclists followed, including a girl on a large tricycle and a very adroit man on a penny-farthing, performing wheelies. Then came a fresh wave of children: young cadets with drums and flutes, and high-stepping pompom girls with twirling batons.

Feeling hungry, I slipped away to Philomena's Restaurant, in Frederick Street North. In this cheerful workmen's café, I enjoyed delicious bright green jelly and ice cream. Men from various parts of Ireland, down for the day, greeted one another with jovial shouts of "What's the story?"

I sat opposite a friendly salesman, a big florid-faced man in a Galway hat, great mutton-chop whiskers, bottle nose and little twinkling eyes. Over my gravy-covered roast, I listened to fond descriptions of his little granddaughter in the west of Ireland.

Later, back on O'Connell Street, I found the parade to be reaching a close. One youth climbed a statue and seemed to be whispering in Parnell's ear. At the Gresham Hotel, the splendid figure of the High Provost of Glasgow hurried to his limousine.

Most incongruous sight of all was that of a crimson-clad American highschool cheerleaders' troop, flown in for the occasion. As they marched through the capital of Ireland, on St Patrick's Day, they chanted over and over again, "Spirit of America! Spirit of America!"

It was time for me to leave Ireland, and this was my cue. But I would return in the summer.

12

A DOLPHIN IN DINGLE

Back in Ireland once more, on a glorious summer's day, I bumped along in a little bus full of Continental students, travelling around the mountains of Dingle, in County Kerry. Dingle is famous for its friendly dolphin, Fungi, who sports among swimmers and boatmen, quite unafraid of mankind. He is never seen with any other dolphins. If he has been banished from the deep sea for some dolphin crime, he's making the best of things.

One of my fellow passengers was Barbara, a Jamaican girl who had travelled all around the world, visiting countries as diverse as Haiti, Lesotho and Mozambique. She was now a teacher in London, with cheerful black British manners.

"I get on very well with Africans—one of my favourite countries is Burkino Faiso," she told me. "If only the people there would have more confidence, and stand up for themselves."

If I had wanted to undermine Barbara's confidence,

I could have told her of many incidences of colour prejudice I had seen in the west of Ireland in my time, even in Cork city itself.

"Sorry, we're just closing!" is a quaint Irish saying often heard as a coloured person enters a bar. Such scenes remind me of 1950s' England, a time when Africans and West Indians were strange to most English people. However, today and yesterday, Dublin gives a friendly welcome to Africans.

"Dingle!" shouted the driver, and I stepped down to the shingle facing the bay. With a jerk, the bus and Barbara shot westward and I saw them no more.

To my disappointment, no golden sand or happy bathers could be seen at Dingle Bay. It was a fjord-like bay, where steep green banks meet a stony shore with hooded crows and a funfair upon it. Bold, good-looking red-headed families hurried in and out of trailer caravans, taking turns to look after the various rides and attractions. The funfair had a slightly ramshackle tinkerish air.

On a moving roundabout car, front paws on the steering wheel, stood a small brown dog dressed in a miniature blouse and skirt. It seemed to be enjoying itself. After a while, a tall barefoot girl with auburn hair picked up the dog and carried it into her caravan.

Wandering on, I saw that a vast tract of Dingle Bay, west of the jetty, was being churned up and concreted, behind an ugly wire fence. A marina was under construction, a sure sign that money without sense had arrived from somewhere. Dolphin revenue may have been partly to blame, for playful Fungi had created a boomtown atmosphere in Dingle. Crowds elbowed me off the pavement almost into the jaws of speeding cars, and I despaired of finding anywhere to stay.

Finally, near the marina, I noticed an unpaved lane known as the Strand. Leading steeply up from the shore, with straggling cottages on each side, the Strand appeared to be a track where boats had been dragged down to the sea. In front of a small white cottage, two Continental students shied away in alarm as a roguish old landlady tried to wheedle them into staying for bed and breakfast. The more she beckoned, chuckled, wheezed and called them "dearie," the more they backed away. Finally they disappeared altogether, so I shot in before the door could close. That's how I got a bed for the next few nights. My hostess introduced herself as Annie Curran, and I made myself at home.

That night, in the town, I roamed the crowded streets in search of Irish music. This I found a-plenty, for musicians from all over County Kerry head for resorts such as Dingle and Killarney in summer. When it grew dark, buskers stood in bright shoplit doorways and twanged, tootled or fiddled. Restaurants were packed, with queues standing outside. This was the only part of Ireland where English holidaymakers could be seen and heard everywhere. Obviously the lure of the Dolphin was stronger than the fear of non-existent bombs. Harassed Hampstead tones rose above the mixed babble of German, French and Danish voices.

Delicious meals were served in bars as well as in restaurants. The Irish bar is far more versatile than the English pub.

By far the best music in Dingle could be heard in O'Flaherty's, the "yobbo" bar, full of rough young people, mostly Irish. Fiddle and flute whirled and blended in a fairy madcap reel. The place was so crowded that I couldn't see the men playing. A little shed or Wendy house stood inside the bar, the door marked "Staff Only." However, it was full of customers sipping drinks and tapping their feet to the music.

A few streets away, a brightly lit bar catered for middle-aged Irish family parties. Children danced to a guitarist and drummer, for wherever Irish people enjoy themselves, their children come too and learn the art of making merry. Switching from Irish balladry to rock and roll, the guitarist produced a trumpet and played in the bygone "showband" style that typified an Irish night out anywhere in the world, twenty years ago.

Everywhere I went, I heard singing and accordion-playing. Fairy lights hung on fishermen's cottages, and voices lilted into microphones.

I'll tell my ma when I get home
The boys won't leave the girls alone.

🍎

Next morning I called on my sister Zenga Longmore at Avondale House (proprietor: Mrs Houlihan). A large neat Victorian building, with delightful stained-glass windows, Mrs Houlihan's guesthouse dominated the corner of Avondale Street. Soon I was wheeling Zenga's two-year-old daughter in a pushchair up the narrow street beside the Avondale to the post office to buy stamps. To the child's delight, we passed an alleyway where the whitewashed walls had been decorated by paintings of cartoon characters. At the post office itself, we admired a stuffed Irish hare in its winter coat, staring at us pop-eyed from its case in the window.

Later, Zenga, Omalara and I strolled around the bay outside the town, avoiding heavy traffic with difficulty. Swallows and yellow wagtails swooped and fluttered.

Leaving the road, we lifted the pushchair over stiles and let the little girl run among cows that chewed the cud and gazed down green banks to blue waters. In the evening, a magic green-tinted light glowed on the headlands. Up on the hill above the town, sleek black snake-headed racehorses showed their paces on the Dingle racetrack. Herons flapped heavily from strand to strand.

Next day, the three of us set off by bus for the lakeside resort of Killarney, the main tourist centre for County Kerry. On the high cliffside at Inch, we admired glorious views over the sea to the mountains on the far side of the bay. Kind teenage girls and small children, all Irish, played happily with Omalara as she darted about the bus. Continental students remained aloof, their knapsacks taking up valuable seat-room. A bumble bee alarmed Omalara. (That sounds like a tongue-twister.) Luckily, a young man killed it when it became entangled in his girlfriend's hair.

Our bus rolled along narrow tunnel-like lanes through

the green shade of overhanging trees. At one corner, we passed a patient grey donkey pulling a flat milk-churn cart. Finally, we arrived at busy Killarney, home of boat trips, coach trips and jaunting-car trips around blue lakes pressed between green mountains. Leaving Zenga and Omalara in their hotel, I made ready to return to Dingle, for our ways were parting. I would soon be off to another western county, no doubt named after somebody's girlfriend, Clare.

Avoiding all the tourist music and razzmatazz, I stopped transfixed outside a dingy little workman's bar, whence dreamlike melancholy music spiralled into the evening air. Inside, I saw a frail old man who held the whole bar silent as he played "Galway Bay" with care and affection. When he had finished, the audience applauded wildly, stamping their enormous boots, yelping and catcalling. I applauded with the rest. Too gentle for a rebel song, the words of "Galway Bay" are yet not wholly complimentary to the English in Ireland:

Oh, the strangers came and tried to teach us their
way,
They scorned us just for being what we are.
They might as well have tried to catch a
moonbeam,
Or light a penny candle from a star...

It was my last day in Dingle, and I set out determined to see the famous dolphin, Fungi. Near the jetty, I noticed a long tarred boat, a currach or elongated sea-going

coracle famous in the annals of old Ireland. Still in use, it lay upside down on a car trailer, ready for launching. A boatman in a shed sold me a ticket for the dolphin excursion boat (a small fishing vessel).

Together with excited camera-wielding families from England and the Continent, we set sail (or set engine, rather) and chugged firmly out into the fjord of Dingle Bay. Mountains loomed in the near distance, and a ruined castle tower stared with its one eye—a window with the light behind it. I now saw that black caves opened into the steep banks above which Omalara and I had wandered, looking at cows.

When the boat steered for the open, middle part of the bay, the waves rose higher, and we bucketed up and down.

"There he is!" someone cried.

I leaped for the side of the boat, just in time to catch a glimpse of a long pale mottled belly swoop below. Fungi swam upside down underneath us, and then soared from the water on the other side of the boat with a graceful arc-like leap. He seemed to enjoy our company, for he dived, leaped, batted his tail on the surface and sometimes sped like a pale torpedo just below the glassy waves. Like all dolphins, he wore a built-in smile, but his dark grey body, with pale patches below and a stubby shark-fin on top, looked wild and whale-like. Performing dolphins in captivity, who do stunts in exchange for fish, look more sleek in their uniform blue-grey bathing suits. Before capture, however, they resembled Fungi. Tank life changes their colour, just as cage life darkens the red breast of a bullfinch.

Suddenly a jovial man sped by in a long currach-like speedboat, cutting a trail of white through the bay. At once, Fungi left us and followed the speedster, charging along directly behind the boat, his body half out of the water. Man and dolphin seemed to wink at one another. Clearly they were old friends.

Well-pleased with all I had seen, I climbed back onto the Dingle jetty. All the same, I prefer seals to whale-kind and feel a greater thrill and a haunting sense of mystery when out after seals in similar waters. But the dolphin appears to be the new sacred "ecological" animal of the English and their American cousins. Dolphin worship alone can lure the English back to Ireland on holiday. It is a far cry today from the Middle Ages, when dolphin and porpoise meat formed prize royal dishes for Friday feasts. The Church deemed the beasts to be fish. Perhaps, in the future, Englishmen will carve dolphin figures on the side of chalk hills, where only horses were carved formerly.

13

ANYONE FOR ENNIS?

One morning I woke up in Annie Curran's bed and breakfast house in Dingle and realised, as my brain slowly stirred to life, that today was the day I was supposed to go to Ennis.

Ennis is the county town of Clare, further north, separated from Kerry by County Limerick and its city namesake.

From my window, I looked down on Annie Curran's backyard, hemmed in by cottage roofs and walls, grey stone and slate. Gardens overflowed with sub-tropical verdancy, flowers, bushes and a plum tree laden with fruit. A stream meandered through the jungle, from the hill to the sea. Black turf, or peat, a reminder of winter, lay neatly stacked on the neighbouring side of the yard wall, roofed over with corrugated iron.

"Next door have a bog," Mrs Curran had informed me, when I first remarked on this. "They cut their own turf and let me have some. Turf is what we burn here in winter, not coal."

Quickly I washed in the small room across the landing, dried myself on the dual-purpose towel that hung across the window on a curtain rail, and hurried downstairs. Annie Curran's bacon, light as a feather, was not to be missed.

"Ah, 'tis a grand morning, so it is," my landlady greeted me, looking more than ever like a large, elderly and benevolent gypsy. "So today you'll be leaving us? Here, wear this medal on a chain and you'll have safe travelling. Look, it shows Our Blessed Lady—the Miraculous Medal."

I wasn't sure where I could find a chain, but I thanked Mrs C politely and put the medal in my pocket. Then I tucked into a sizzlingly delicious breakfast, to the sound of a jig-crazed fiddle wafting from the record player in Mrs Curran's dark cavern of an old-fashioned kitchen.

After a lengthy goodbye, in the course of which I promised to spread the fame of kindly Annie Curran's guesthouse far and wide, I ran from the Strand and towards the waiting bus for Tralee. Plastic bag of belongings by my side, I nestled in a window seat and looked out at the view.

Dingle's natural harbour, hemmed in by hills, was soon left behind. As the dark red single-decker climbed into the hills, I looked out on high hedges ablaze with fuchsia blossoms, scarlet as berries. Suddenly tropical red would be replaced by vivid orange, for another garden flower, montbretia, has also grown into an Irish hedge. Kerry's flowering hedges, where humming birds and giant butterflies would not look amiss, form a pleasant contrast with the bare green hills beyond the roads. Even there, among sheep and broken dry stone walls, the pink heather manages to look Amazonian. Black strips on the hillside show where turf has been removed for fuel.

Eventually the little bus entered the town of Tralee, by way of a causeway-like road that seemed to run along the centre of a river, seagulls on each side. Outside Tralee railway station, I leaped ahead of back-packing young Scandinavians, and rode off on another bus to Limerick city. Scandinavian tourists force everyone else to take up the Scandinavian sport of queue-jumping. Before long, we (that is, Scandinavians, a few squashed Irish and I) had reached the substantial town of Newcastle West.

As the bus travelled northward into County Limerick, the magical scenery of Kerry faded away. Gently rolling pasturelands became prosaic and English, native hedges replaced Amazonia and shepherds with flocks of sheep and rams no longer barred our way. In some fields the hay had evidently been cut and baled by machinery. Instead of stacking the slabs of hay into high-rise blocks, as in England, the farmers had dotted them about the fields like Kerry haycocks, in little three-bale lean-to card-houses. Clubheaded bullrushes grew in hundreds by riverside marshes.

Sometimes the fields seemed neglected, growing neater where farms had formed part of a big estate. Ruined lodge houses and broken gates spoke sadly of a time that was gone. Adare, a lordly Anglo-Irish town near Limerick, was particularly splendid. A castle and a mansion peeped over demesne walls, and town houses

Irish Travellers

boasted newly thatched roofs of palest gold. The former lord's park was now being used as both a golf and race course. Another change of buses and I found myself crossing the wide River Shannon. At last, bus and I entered Clare, county of mystery. Irish travelling people abounded north of Limerick, particularly where roads were being widened or factories built. Like Romany gypsies, tinkers thrive best in the twilight zone where industry and agriculture meet. They seemed a vigorous people, roaring at one another from off-white trailer doorways. One curly-haired young man whipped his horse to a gallop and raced along a piece of unmade road, pulling a flat milk-churn cart on which a row of children bounced happily. In Kerry, such carts had been drawn by meek farm donkeys.

Bunratty Castle loomed grandly by the roadside. A few more twists and turns of the road, and there I was at Ennis, once more outside a railway station. An old steam engine, now a gigantic ornament, rested in a siding at Ennis Station. I walked through suburbia into town, and eventually found a place to stay, at Walnut House, in Turnpike Road.

Peter Fitzgerald, the effusive landlord, spoke eloquently of the wonders of County Clare, his voice muffled by a thick moustache. For some reason, he referred to his small hotel as a "hostel." To me it seemed more like a cross between an American motel and a conservatory, with more than a pinch of Irish craft shop thrown in. Entrance was through a flower-and-motto-ridden glasshouse, every inch of the walls covered in pictures, posters or trailing plants.

Elderly but active, talkative Mr Fitzgerald abounded in friendliness and energy, and seemed to take great interest in local affairs. I unpacked, then hurried out to explore. As I left, I noticed the framed photographs of heroes of Irish Independence near the kitchen door—de Valera and grim Michael Collins ("The Big Fellow").

Seldom had I met an Irish town as delightful as Ennis. From the Walnut House on the outskirts of town, a long narrow street of bright well-kept little shops, bars and cafés ran downhill to the town centre, passing the tall grey Catholic cathedral. Evening was drawing on, but the pavements were filled with cheerful people, going in and out of doorways and stepping carefully around one another. One reason why the ancient stone pavements were crowded was because they were so narrow, scarcely more than a yard in width. Streets still followed the town's mediaeval plan. However, most of the present shops and houses had been built during the past two hundred years.

Long, twisty O'Connell Street snaked on its way. I gave a gasp of admiration as an immense classical statue on top of an enormous pillar of stone came into view, marking the end of the street. It was as if a Roman monument had survived intact in the midst of Tudor London. High on top of the pillar stood a noble Roman senator, complete with flowing toga and a lightning conductor on his head. Closer inspection revealed him to be Daniel O'Connell ("The Liberator"), the tireless and successful fighter for Catholic Emancipation. "The

Derrynane," a dark mahogany bar, hotel and tea-house near the statue's plinth, had been named after the house (and townland) where O'Connell was born in 1775. When O'Connell died, in the famine year of 1847, Ireland's stern grey Victorian heritage of Catholic institutions was well established and growing fast.

Column and statue had been raised on the very spot where O'Connell had addressed an outdoor meeting in 1828. Forty years after that memorable meeting, the statue stood completed. In his early life, O'Connell had been a fiery man, who had fought and won duels. It seemed only fitting that lightning would be drawn to the head of one who had once electrified vast crowds with his eloquence.

A placard at the column's base, abandoned by successful hitch-hikers, read "Ennis or Near, Please. We're Late for Work." Hitch-hiking is an acceptable way of travel in Ireland, the mainstay of many a commuter.

Four narrow roads of bright shopfronts and doorways radiated from the tall monument. I followed my nose, ambling downhill to a large ruined Franciscan friary and onwards to the wide, dark River Fergus. A curving riverside walk led me 'neath the avenues of trees to a Georgian town hall. Not much further on, Ennis ended and farmland began. I doubled back into town, discovering tall red-brick Dublin-style eighteenth-century houses. These faced an unkempt field which sloped down to the black bubbling river. White ducks and geese were kept here, the river their pond, for they never swam far from home.

On the opposite shore from the ducks, lovers strolled along the prom. An archway led from an open car park to yet another narrow sloping street. Ignoring tantalising alleys, I walked along, glancing into shop windows until I reached a jutting-out corner shop, Guerin's, with a knobbly bollard-like stone outside the door.

A naïve painting on the shop wall showed the same scene as it had been in Victorian times. A larger stone, beside the first one, acted as a seat for a fiddle-player. Old and young, in the picture, danced merrily. Instead of Guerin, the writing above the shop window read D Murphy.

With a shock of delight, I realised that I had stumbled upon a place celebrated in Irish song. Johnny Patterson, an exile in America, composed "The Stone Outside Dan Murphy's Door" in a fit of homesickness for Ennis and his lost childhood. Patterson's widow, I am told, is still alive and dwelling in Liverpool.

Humming Patterson's homely ditty to myself, I returned to the town centre, where hundreds of jackdaws flew squawking overhead in the failing light.

Dan Murphy would bring down the fiddle,
While his daughter looked after the store,
And music would ring to the songs we would sing
On the stone outside Dan Murphy's door.

In a bar-cum-café, I ordered a pot of tea and admired a charming Japanese family at the next table. A row of children, not much smaller than their diminutive parents, all sat licking ice cream cones. Foreign holidaymakers had not yet reached plague proportions in Ennis, and so the locals regarded them with kindly interest, often striking up conversations. In Dingle, tourists had overwhelmed the town and made the native Dinglians invisible. I had been told that every winter, many able-bodied west of Ireland men went abroad and worked in bars, returning like swallows each spring. Conversation at a nearby table in the Ennis café confirmed this story. A big pleasant-faced young man had been welcomed back to Ireland by affectionate relatives. He told them of his adventures, and they hung on every word.

"I served in one of the biggest pubs in Australia—it had seven bars. All the customers were Hungarian and Czech car workers from the huge factory next door. I'm telling you, they were a highly dangerous crowd. Men couldn't have handled them, but brisk barmaids kept them in order."

It was dark when I emerged from the bar-café, but the friary, town hall and O'Connell monument were all brightly floodlit. Cheerful young people roamed the streets in twos and threes, dipping into bar after bar. All seemed good-natured. Young couples held hands and kissed, looking very innocent. Whenever a youth felt overcome with drink, he would sit down in a shop doorway. Live rock groups alternated with traditional *céilí* bands in many pubs. In one crowded bar, I tapped my feet to the music of an accordionist and a dark-eyebrowed young fiddle player.

To my consternation, I saw a white-faced girl of about

twelve sitting in a doorway vomiting piteously. A friend who sat by her side grew tired of comforting her, and walked sharply away, brisk as an Australian barmaid.

"What's the trouble here?" I asked.

"My friend's sick, but it's her own fault. There's a lot of drugs about, here in Ennis."

So youthful matters were not as innocent as they had seemed.

Back at the Walnut House, landlord Peter Fitzgerald showed me his family photographs framed on the wall.

"That's my mother when she was in her prime," he sighed, pointing at the portrait of a dignified lady of faintly tragic expression. My eyes fell on Peter's black tie, and he said he was in mourning for his late brother.

Whispers and bumbling noises of other returning guests amused me by their over-cautiousness as I sat reading in my room.

🍎

Next day, I set off for the Ennis Agricultural Show at the edge of town. At first, I took a wrong turning and found myself in a sprawling council estate. I could see the crowds and the showground beyond the rooftops. Some of the new houses had been built in the severe wine-red Gothic style of modern Toxteth, in Liverpool, and looked quite attractive. Home-made "No Vehicles" signs were everywhere, and in one cul-de-sac near the playground, parked cars had been arranged as a barrier, perhaps to prevent travellers from crashing their lorries through into the show. Two red-haired traveller boys ran up to me and asked for "change." Their faces were freckled into giraffe patterns, delicate traceries of pale skin colour between massive blotches of orange.

"You can easily climb over the wall and get into the show," a housewife cheerfully informed me.

Through a barred and padlocked gate, I could see sleek black racehorses carry riders effortlessly over the "jumps." Ennis Show seemed devoted entirely to displays of horsemanship. After looking at the wall for a long time, I decided that the housewife had overestimated my agility. So I walked around.

A cattle sale had just ended, but show-jumping was in full swing. Most of the horses in the main outdoor ring belonged to the local hunts, and leaped over barriers in great style. Friendly family crowds watched attentively, while others formed little circles for gossip. Farmers were less red-faced and wind-ravaged than their rugged Kerry counterparts, for Ennis is set in lush buttercup countryside. Judges and their Ascot-hatted wives obviously belonged to a highly convivial and jokey "county set."

Indoors, in an auction ring, other horses were put through their paces. Upstairs, the over-packed bar seemed to strain at the seams, as if about to burst and shower drinkers over the field. Outside I roamed around a city or camp of horseboxes, where children played uproariously. Some youngsters sat protectively beside the legs of their family horse. Roars of approval came from the crowd, as harrier and foxhunter horses showed their mettle. Loudspeakers crackled and bugles tooted, the latter instruments held high by dare-devil riders.

"And now a lap of honour from the County Clares! There they go!"

Scraps of earth scudded from pounding hooves as the Clares did their stuff. Some of the riders wore black, others hunting pink.

Prizes were then presented by Sergeant Major Hickey, and we all walked home, eating hot dogs or licking ice creams.

🍎

A strange limestone tableland, the Burren looms high on the horizon, a few miles outside Lisdoonvarna in County Clare. Naturalists from far and wide visit the Burren to study the strange creatures that make their home there. On one rainy day, shortly after my arrival in Clare, a very strange creature indeed could be seen straggling along the road to Lisdoonvarna. This was myself, hoping against hope that I could catch the last bus to Ennis and return safely to the warmth of Walnut House.

Outside a modern house by the road, three big men were shovelling gravel from one pile to another. A savage sweep of rain sent them scurrying into the house for cover. To my surprise, one of them beckoned me over with a shout.

"Come and shelter!" he roared, and I obeyed.

Within five minutes I found myself sitting at a table in a half-decorated room, a mug of tea and a slab of cake in front of me. So this was Burren hospitality!

All three men proved to be lorry drivers, and the one who had saved me from the rain introduced himself as Gerry "Donkey" Dobbin from Belfast. He was a cheerful young man in his thirties, with a scrubby black moustache untouched by Guinness or porter, for Gerry was a teetotaller.

"I do the Shannon Airport to Moscow run, loading up with duty free at Shannon and driving clear across Europe to the duty free shop at Moscow Airport," he told me. "It's a hard run, that. You see, the Moscow people can't manage to stock their own duty free, so they have made a trade agreement with Ireland."

My mind boggled slightly at the thought of Paddy whiskey and shamrock tea-towels on sale in Russia. Gerry knew London very well, and we swapped anecdotes. Before long, all four of us in the half-completed house were animatedly discussing fiddle players who had sold their souls to the devil.

"The bus to Ennis leaves the square at Lisdoonvarna in about five minutes," Gerry observed, to my consternation. "I'll just wrap you up some cake for your journey and drive you down there."

He was as good as his word, for just as the single-decker bus rolled into the square, Gerry and I arrived on the scene and I jumped from one vehicle to another. Waving goodbye, Gerry sped back to the gravel. A watery sun appeared and the rain stopped falling.

"This is the famous Doolin!" the driver announced, as he pulled into a small black village where green misty fields sloped down towards a pale grey sea.

"Famous Doolin!" repeated a Japanese knapsack-girl with a shy laugh, a hand across her mouth. Many young backpackers left the bus, some to climb into the bare rugged hills, others to descend to a harbour. A ferry boat crossed from Doolin to Inis Oírr, one of the Aran Islands. Now the bus was almost empty. Remaining passengers were nearly all Irish.

"Doolin's musicians are famous all over Ireland," someone remarked. "That's what the Continentals all come here for."

Sleepily, I listened to the driver shouting to a crony in Welsh. The crony, a stout chaffing old man, who could have been a fisherman or a farmer, shouted back in the same harsh language. Suddenly I realised that I was in Ireland, not in Cardiganshire! I had been listening to Gaelic spoken as a living tongue!

Before long we were off again, along the tops of the Cliffs of Moher and skirting the Hog's Head on the road to Liscannor. Misty upland on one side of the road, the sea far below on the other. Long white breakers coursed the whole grey Atlantic Ocean. There were no trees in this windswept country. Here and there, neat white cottages with golden thatched roofs stood beside the stone-walled fields. In most parts of Ireland, cottages have long been ruins. Here they were lived in. Even one run-down cottage with grass growing from the sagging roof had a plume of turf-smoke rising from the chimney.

An Irish cottage is a little one-storey two-window house with thick stone walls. The front door opens into a kitchen, as a rule, and there is a living and sleeping room at each end. Sometimes the top half of the front door opens, to serve as a window. All over the Celtic world, such cottages are falling into disuse. There is a larger version, with a loft bedroom reached by a ladder and an end room for livestock. A shutter sometimes opens to connect the parlour with the cow byre.

Near Lahinch, a high grassy ridge hid the sea. A moment later, we crossed a bridge over the wide estuary of the River Cullenagh, with its sandy beaches, gulls and waterfowl. For a time, the river seemed to run parallel to the sea, before it opened out into Liscannor Bay. Rugged tussocky dune-like landscape had been converted into golf-courses. Lush farmland appeared after we had passed the town of Ennistymon, a foretaste of Ennis.

Just then, to my consternation, five drunk brawling young men, all large and muscular, tumbled swearing into the bus. Flinging themselves onto seats around me, they began to roar football slogans. I soon gathered that they supported Glasgow Celtic. Other passengers stiffened and stared out the window. Four of the young men looked decent enough beneath the bravado. They were Irish, but the steely-eyed ringleader was Glasgow-Irish over on holiday with his cousins. Very drunk, he boldly sat next to a young girl who was travelling on her own, and tried to chat her up. However, she seemed well able to look after herself, and sent him crestfallen to a seat behind me, where he breathed heavily on my neck.

"Baldy! Yer —ing baldy!" he chanted.

I am bald as an egg. Do you think he was trying to

be personal? In similar circumstances, the prophet Elisha
had called up she-bears. The Irish bear has gone the way
of the Irish wolf, so I was forced instead to draw pictures
of Bugs Bunny in my notepad, with a view to ingratiating
myself with the youth.

"I hate the —ing English, do you know that?" the
youth kept repeating, in a maddening monotone. "Do
you *know* that? English baldy!"

"Shut up, you're a baldy yourself!" one of his friends
remonstrated. "You're a gyp from a —ing caravan."

At this, the whole lot of them began to sing. It is a
curiosity of Ireland that yobbo youths love traditional
music. Tapes of jigs and reels play in Space Invader
arcades. "Whack fol de daddy-o," the youths warbled.
"Rare bog, rattling bog!" Finally they settled for an
interminable ditty called "In Our Neighbourhood."

Then they began to tussle among themselves in rowdy
horseplay. The Glasgow-Irish boy sat next to me and
drew on a cigarette.

"I hate the English, do you *know* that?" he queried.

"Have a picture of Bugs Bunny," I proffered.

"Is that for *me*? You're the only decent Englishman
I've ever met!" he shouted.

Another boy asked for a drawing of a mutant turtle
on his plaster-cast arm, so I obliged. I had to parry some
awkward questions about beer and football teams, and
endure a certain amount of urine on the floor, but I got
to Ennis safe and sound. My knowledge of Irish songs
helped, and so did the fact that the Glaswegian and I
turned out both to be acquaintances of Peter Cannon,

the disc jockey of Donegal town. At Ennis, the youths leaped whooping into a friend's car and vanished. So I strolled down to the O'Connell statue and bade Ennis a peaceful goodbye.

14

1992: DUBLIN AGAIN

Yes, I was back in Dublin, but what a different Dublin! This time, through no fault of my own, I found myself among geniuses. This witty hard-drinking literary set frequent the Shelbourne Hotel on St Stephen's Green. The enormous hotel, with figures of Nubian princesses and slave girls at the steps to welcome you into a glittering Edwardian-style Bohemia, had become a centre for journalists, critics, authors, screenplay-writers and weekly columnists. One person could easily accommodate all these roles at once. Girl-geniuses seemed particularly good at this kind of thing. Talk flew from their lips at the rate of ten epigrams a second, leaving me stunned. The barman cashed literary-advance cheques nonchalantly.

"Who's publishing your novel about the missing soul-singing bishop?" I asked one cheque-waving débutante.

"Oh, I haven't got a publisher! It's really a screenplay. You see, novelists get tax exemption in this country, didn't you know? So when someone wants a screenplay

The Horseshoe Bar, Shelbourne Hotel, Dublin

it gets commissioned as a novel."

That explained a great deal about Irish writing—many novels looked exactly like film scripts, the book of the film written before the film. Although I could hardly hear her in the packed bar where blue smoke matched the conversation, she began to speak faster and faster about her personal life in all its indiscretions. Male geniuses are particularly good at making their own scandalous behaviour the subject of their columns. If Dickens were alive today in the bar of the Shelbourne, he would be perpetually on the telephone to a copy-editor about his affair with an actress and the shabby way he treated his wife.

Thanks to the kindness of two or three geniuses, I had been loaned a room in Harcourt Street, one of the great Georgian thoroughfares near St Stephen's Green. Out of gratitude, I felt obliged to pop into the Shelbourne and wave at my benefactors through the crowd. All the same, I did so warily. On one occasion, a man from the *Cork Examiner* cornered me and took me to task over a passage in my book *Jaunting Through Ireland*.

"Why did you say that the people of west Cork have Welsh accents?" he demanded angrily. "Why not say that Welsh people had west Cork accents?"

At the time, I had been lost for words, for he had a good point there. Ogham writing on Welsh standing stones shows that many parts of west Wales had been settled by the Irish of ancient times. The Welsh are by no means all the descendants of Romano-Britons and the heirs of Rome. On the pig's ear of north Wales, the

Lleyn peninsula is said to have been named by settlers from the Irish province of Leinster.

Stifled by the creative atmosphere of the Shelbourne, I sipped out for a nostalgic visit to O'Brien's Hotel on the north side. Taxi drivers, I had found, asked "Which side?" when you jumped in. North of the river was unfashionable, the exact opposite of London. Harcourt Street was very south side.

Almost on the steps of the hotel, I was stopped by two young Russians who opened their jackets to reveal bottles of vodka, "only four pounds." All over the West, Russians are now selling, or trying to sell, items of every kind. Probably the secret stores of luxury goods reserved "for members of the Party only" have now been looted. Talking of economics, I was pleased to see that the Irish and English pounds had now reached a state of friendly equality. Soon, London taxi drivers may prefer to be paid in Irish money.

At the corner entrance to St Stephen's Green, Dublin's Marble Arch, I headed down Grafton Street towards the river. One of the Shelbourne crowd had told me that this arch, raised to honour the Irish dead who fought for Britain in the Boer War, is known as Traitors' Gate. The nickname commemorates the time when the patriots of 1916 had regarded the Boers' struggle for independence as a symbol of their own hopes. Nowadays, the Boers seem more closely to resemble diehard Orangemen.

In Grafton Street, I paused at the edge of a large crowd and found that it was circled around a boy of eight who flailed savagely at a guitar and sang rock'n'roll songs in an angry monotone, an expression of un-changing unspeakable ferocity on his face. Coins flew into his cap, as he danced with rage, never pausing. At last he did pause, and I asked him his name.

"Joseph," he replied shortly. "Well, it's a-one for the money, two for the show..."

There you have it—Joseph. Mark well that name, reader, for Joseph will be famous some day.

When I reached O'Brien's Hotel, proprietor Maureen O'Sullivan welcomed me into her Victorian parlour (off-limits to guests) for a cup of tea. She and her sister had just returned from a trip to South Africa, where a relative helped to organise "black trade unions."

"We drove all over the country, to places where white people never go," Maureen told me. "In Ciscei we met a troop of naked men, painted white. They may have been returning from an initiation ceremony."

(Such ceremonies bind together an age-group with sacred vows. In some parts of Africa, one initiate out of each group never returns, his fate sealed by a vow of silence. Once initiated, the age-group usually become model citizens.)

"We really admired the Africans—they were so artistic," her sister put in. "They decorate their huts with lovely patterns, and make intricate pictorial tapestries. But in the towns they were quite different! Instead of smiles and laughter, they greeted us with ironic Black Power salutes. It was a bit frightening."

I began to take notes, explaining that I was going to put their hotel into a book.

"Titled people have been here," I was told. "But now we get mainly backpackers. Kitty Kiernan stayed here once—she used to be the fiancée of the patriot, Michael Collins."

Tearing myself away with reluctance, I emerged into a rainy night and hurried back to Harcourt Street.

Although it was late, I noticed that Bewley's, the famous tea and bun shop in Grafton Street, was still open. Always crowded, the large Victorian café now stayed open until two in the morning! It has its own museum, the only uncrowded part, where I sometimes go to eat buns. If only Bewley's had no customers, I could discover Pre-Raphaelite wonders there, but as it is, it's like Heuston Station in the rush hour. So I forged on to Harcourt Street.

🍎

On my first morning in my strange new surroundings, I opened the wooden shutters of the bow window and gazed out onto the back garden of a strange dwelling used by nuns. In a central niche stood a white statue of a Twenties flapper in a dressing gown. To her right and left, white lions hung casually out of portholes, their paws dangling. Behind the slate roof and chimneypots of this edifice, the grey stone wall of a stately park could be seen. Apparently this park, with its statues, caves and dried-up pools, is attached to University College, Dublin, at Earlsfort Terrace and Stephen's Green. Unknown to the public, the park is open to it.

Out in Harcourt Street, I found an arched entry in the long swathe of white-pillared Georgiana, and made a zigzag journey to the city centre. A strange tower drew me towards Adelaide Road, a leafy red-brick thoroughfare, where I discovered an ornate and unashamedly imperial hospital, the Royal Victorian Eye and Ear, complete with lion and unicorn. Retracing my steps, I headed along proletarian Aungier Street, with its heavy traffic, old shops and menacing council flats. Dublin is no respecter of persons. In the city centre, there appear to be no exclusive quarters for rich, poor or middle people. In terms of Monopoly cards, Mayfair, Whitechapel and Wimbledon have been dealt out side by side. Has a Dublin Monopoly game been invented? If so, I would like to see it.

Near a stripped-pine YMCA full of French girls, I came across the neo-Gothic doorway of an immense church attached to the Carmelite fraternity, a group of monks and priests. On a step, beside a stone engraved "Refuge of Sinners; Pray for Us," a dignified white-haired old lady sat begging, holding out a wicker basket. I accepted the invitation for refuge, and after looking at the church, explored the late-Victorian Carmelite corridors. Colour photographs on the walls showed happy African babies being helped by concerned Carmelites. After a late breakfast in the oak-panelled coffee shop, I strayed into the monastery garden, where a fountain tinkled among the roses and a crucifix looked on.

Out in the street once more, I paused to allow a heavily blinkered nag to pull a flat cart out of an alleyway. The driver and his friend carried a small cargo of slates.

Even more than most cities, Dublin was made for the horse. Unhappy with motor cars, the streets still seem to miss their old friends, for horse and donkey traffic dominated Ireland until the 1950s. Without horses, Dublin would be aimless and senseless. Luckily, there are still a few horses around.

Further into town, in South Great George's Street, I stopped enchanted at the window of the Doll Hospital and Store. What wonderful dolls, with frilly bonnets or Oriental costumes, and grave two-year-old faces! If only I had my niece Omalara here, and a thousand pounds in my pocket!

Across the road, in a railway-like arcade of clean red brick, the stalls of South City Market tempted browsers to become shoppers. If I had not been broke as usual, I might have come home with a pocketful of parrots from the old-fashioned pet shop. This whole market is now up for sale, lock, stock and parakeet.

Emerging from narrow, enticing streets to Trinity College, I came across an accordion player. She wore a loud green velvet hat with a feather, and a shawl and dress to match, pinned with a Tara brooch. A box of faded photographs and postcards was at her side, on the plinth of a statue. Her face was florid, expressive, dark-eyed and beaming.

"Yes, I'm a scholar and a philosopher," she was saying to an earnest man in a heavy grey suit. "So is my present husband. As for the first one, I had to learn to take a punch here and a hit there. I can play music from any part of the world, not just from Ireland."

Evidently she had been playing "Kevin Barry," one of the tunes that lured me to Ireland. In a harsh Dublin accent, her patron said that a warden had played him a tape of Kevin speaking in Mountjoy Jail, on the eve of the young rebel's execution. Did they have tapes in 1920, I wondered?

"From what I heard from Kevin's niece, the Barry family was very upset about the whole affair," the man continued. "They always wanted him to finish his medical studies."

"My name is Eileen Chevalier," the accordion lady told me proudly, when the friend of the Barrys had departed. "I guess you're from England, so I'll play you a Yorkshire tune, 'Linden Lea.'"

Halfway through, she switched to a lively reel from Scotland, "Marie's Wedding."

"I know that's not very English," she admitted, "but a lot of lads from Liverpool ask for it."

An urbane Nigerian, with a humorous face, then arrived, and listened to her claims of being able to play "any music."

"I'm a doctor now working in America," he said. "I specialise in voodoo. (That's a joke.) Can you play a Muddy Waters tune?"

"Certainly not—I'll play you 'Old Man River' by Paul Robeson," Eileen told him sternly, holding up a photograph of the star in question.

"He's old-fashioned! I want Muddy Waters."

"*All* black people like Paul Robeson," she informed him firmly, and began to play.

I left them to it, crossed Trinity and found myself for the first time in my life in wondrous Kildare Street, the South Kensington and Westminster of Dublin. Here stood imposing Leinster House, much-guarded seat of government, with museums in annexes and side buildings.

I entered the imposing foyer of the National Museum, where perspectives were marred by makeshift modern displays. Just like a London museum, in fact. This museum seemed dedicated to the proposition that nothing worth preserving had been found in Ireland between the arrival and departure of the English. So displays jumped straight from gold torques and Viking fragments to the *actual clothes and guns* used by the rebels of 1916 and 1920. Effete tragic-eyed white tailor dummies posed in rebels' uniforms like French mime artists. Admittedly, this was a temporary exhibition, with other displays housed elsewhere, and the museum was nearly empty.

All the same, I found exhibits more to my taste in the large Natural History Museum, nearby. Gigantic skeletons of bog-preserved Irish elks loomed across the entrance hall, painted shiny black. This set the sombre tone of a museum that seemed scarcely to have changed in the past century. Row upon row of cases stood tightly packed with stuffed animals, a memorial to an age when naturalist-sportsmen could scarcely rest until they had killed one member of every single species of animal in a continent. Between them, they had filled two floors and side galleries of the large museum. Many of the exhibits reminded me of old natural history books of the 1900s, when woodcuts were being replaced by photographs. Instead of quaint drawings, such books showed photos of sad-looking stuffed animals with large misshapen heads and glass eyes a size too small. Most of the creatures here in Dublin resembled those illustrations, the Irish animals excepted. Greater care had been lavished upon Hibernian birds and beasts, and a rare jet-black common seal presented a most striking appearance.

Upstairs, among the foreign animals, complete skeletons of large beasts such as camels were on open display, guarded from curious children by jovial keepers. Cheerful keepers seemed not altogether incongruous in such a setting, for the skeleton of a rhino also seemed to be in high spirits, if not laughing. I was interested to see the knobbles of its spine rising into spikes to support the animal's hump-like shoulders.

One technique of the taxidermists of old Ireland must be unique—the device of putting a ready-mounted animal-head face upwards on the floor of a landscaped case, among tufty grass, so it would look as if it were sinking into a bog. This would explain why it had no body. In one case, two wild dogs fought savagely over a stag that seemed to be sinking before their eyes. If they didn't hurry and make up their minds, neither of them would get it!

Another landscaped display showed a full-bodied African lion cruelly ignoring the fate of its comrade, who stared up beseechingly from a bog, only its face visible. "Will nobody save me?" the poor lion seemed to be saying.

Surfeited at last, I returned to Harcourt Street.

Harcourt Street itself, a living museum of Georgian Dublin, seemed worthy of study. Beginning with the house where I was staying, I counted a gargoyle over the front door, two eagles on the stairs that had lost their heads in 1916, and more stone or plaster columns and rococo twiddles than I would care to mention. Tables and dressers inside had clawed feet, a style known as Irish grotesque. Oriental writing on next door's window denoted the presence of the Chinese Chamber of Commerce. As with all streets of tall urban Georgian dwellings, no one building contained one family. Everything behind the front doors had been divided and subdivided into flats, basements and offices.

Somebody at the Shelbourne advised me to go to Newman House, two Georgian buildings that had been merged into one, in 1865, in order to house the newly formed Catholic University of Ireland. The former haunt of celebrated Cardinal Newman, first rector of the university, had been turned into a "stately home" (admittance one pound). Once, while wandering through Oxford, I had come across the overturned statue of Cardinal Newman gathering moss in a forgotten corner of college shrubbery. Probably he had been laid low by an Anglican who could not forgive his turning to Rome.

Feeling sorry for Newman, I set off to pay him honour and also to see a Catholic curiosity—a buxom figure of Juno clothed in a fur coat slapped on by the Jesuits when they first took over the aristocratic house. Thinking the house to be in Harcourt Street, I rang the doorbell at the correct number and was admitted by a buzzer to a glorious eighteenth-century hallway and staircase, the lavish stucco ornamentation picked out in vivid blue or white paint. After a puzzled interview with a young lady on the stairs, I realised I was in a private house (actually a student hostel) by mistake, and hastily left. Almost any door picked at random in Harcourt or Fitzwilliam Streets, or on St Stephen's Green, would reveal a stately home.

Other oddities of Harcourt Street included a Celtic Bookshop, where the elegant lady manager spoke to one and all in refined Gaelic, and a redundant railway station. It was a pity that noble Harcourt Street Station, with its grey classical façade, had to be closed in the 1960s because it was the fashion. However, it's an ill-wind, for the station vaults have been acquired by Findlaters, the grocers turned wine-merchants, and turned into an enormous series of echoing cash-and-carry wine cellars. One of the vaults contained a Findlaters Museum, similar to Bewley's Café museum—a celebration of the merchants of old Dublin who are still around today. Like many nineteenth-century merchant families, the Findlaters were Presbyterians. On my visit I admired the boneshaker messenger-bikes, the old photographs and the beautifully curved sweeps of ceiling within these railway catacombs. A rubicund Findlater appeared from an office and gave me a friendly nod.

Towards the end of my stay, I came across a row in Harcourt Street. A group of rowdy young people, tall curly-headed young men and red-haired girls with defiant eyes, were stamping and jumping around in a circle, outside a grand front door. Two gardaí watched over them in wary amusement. Uttering cheerful bellows, the young people waved placards that read "Youth Defence" and "Abortion Kills Youth."

A very young girl grew tired, lay down her placard and sat on a kerbstone. I asked her what it was all about.

"We are pro-life," she told me readily, "and a famous doctor who is anti-life lives in that house. We're letting him know what we think of him."

"Is he there now? Won't he come out?" I asked.

"He's in there all right, but he won't come out!"

"In England, young people who protest are on the doctor's side," I said.

"Well, we want to show the world that *all* young people aren't like that."

"I think you're disgusting!" a well-dressed woman addressed the throng.

"Slut!" shouted one of the pro-life men in a jeering tone.

This unhappy scene notwithstanding, the pro-life people seemed to be on the losing side in Dublin. Among the Shelbourne geniuses, the nation's opinion-makers, the Catholic Church was looked upon as an oppressor, or at best a comic bogeyman. As with the British royal family, indiscretions within the Church had contributed to this new unpopularity. All over Ireland, bright young people have grown up on a diet of English and American pop music and television. John Waters's book, *Jiving at the Crossroads*, describes provincial young people who earnestly seek enlightenment and wider horizons in the pages of the London-based rock newspaper, *New Musical Express*.

Why do I, an Englishman, not feel more pleased when I contemplate an Ireland that turns from thoughts of martyrs, rebels and separation from England towards the international youthful dream of abortions, contraceptives, drugs and fashions? The institution that separates Ireland from England, the Catholic Church, is already being spoken of in scathing terms once reserved for the Protestant Ascendancy. I'm all for friendship and accord between Ireland and England, but not at the cost of reviving anti-Papism and the Penal Laws. Will Ireland always be Ireland?

🍎

All such gloomy thoughts were banished on my last day in Ireland, a day of pure ecstasy, a visit to Dublin Zoo! Now a Dublin Zoo celebrity, a contributor to the Fellows' magazine, *Dublin Zoo Matters*, I was met near the entrance by the enthusiastic director, Peter Wilson. He gave me a guided tour, and even unlocked the hippo house for my benefit. There I saw a charming pink-faced hippo piglet, only a few days old yet already smiling. Hippos have a built-in smile.

Before my eyes, the huge mother hippopotamus submerged to the bottom of her indoor pool, followed by the youngster, who fastened on and began to suck milk underwater. The baby's head was concealed by the mother's bulging flank, but the rapidly filling body was visible, the little legs trembling with satisfaction. Every now and then the baby came up to breathe, looking at me with the curious, frank expression of an Irish child.

Director and I shared our fantasies of an ideal zoo and found them identical. We both wanted underwater viewing chambers for polar bears and hippos, giant aquariums for mammals.

"At Denver Zoo, Colorado, the hippos can be seen underwater through a glass window," the director said excitedly. "They have a very good filtration system, of course. Did you know that hippos don't swim so much as run along the bottom of lakes and rivers?"

Big cat cages had been combined into one large enclosure for a sprightly young snow leopard, who swiped energetically at a suspended punchbag. On a tree-filled island, the great black siamang ape boomed with an extended throat-sack, a grey balloon that swelled and shrank with each whooping note. A high-pitched note accompanied each boom, like bagpipes and Lambeg drum in Belfast. Two furry youngsters wrestled and tussled in the leafy branches. Around the island, wild coots with bobbing heads swam urgently on the dark lake waters.

"Won't you let me go inside one of the cages?" I begged. "What about the python tank? I love holding pythons."

"Our reptile house is closed," Peter Wilson said regretfully. "But I'll see what I can do."

What he did was this. He called the monkey-house keeper and arranged for me to go inside the large cage of the ring-tailed lemurs. From outside the bars, these silver-grey Madagascar cat-monkeys, with black and white racoon heads and tails, seemed a somnolent lot. They huddled together, half-asleep on the grass, ignoring the forest of dead trees and branches arranged in the large cage for their exercise.

"These animals bite!" a notice proclaimed.

"That's only a precaution!" the roguish red-faced keeper laughed. Later I found that he often allowed attractive young lady visitors to frolic with the lemurs.

As soon as I went inside, the graceful animals sprang joyously onto my head, arms and shoulders. They seemed genuinely pleased to see me. When their interest waned, I tempted them back with a banana. How soft their dark hands seemed, as they gravely examined my head! How lovely their soft grey fur, suffused with just a touch of reddish-brown, how lithe and long their limbs! Enchanted, I walked around a lemur fairyland, as the dark-eyed animals ran along the branches and stared at me keenly.

Surely Ireland was Paradise!

ALSO BY ROY KERRIDGE

Beside the Seaside and Other Tales
The Store's Outing
Druid Madonna
Real Wicked, Guy
The Lone Conformist
Bizarre Britain
In the Deep South
Jaunting Through Ireland

WHAT THE CRITICS SAID ABOUT ROY KERRIDGE'S PREVIOUS BOOK, *JAUNTING THROUGH IRELAND*

"He has a gift of being able to see everything while not appearing to be looking at all."

Muriel Bolger, *Irish Press*

"Well written, superbly observed."

Eugene McGloin, *Longford Leader*

"A...somewhat quirky intelligence that delights the listener and will charm the reader."

Catherine Murphy, *Evening Herald*

"Kerridge has the ability to see everyday life with a fresh eye."

Jeffrey Klinke, *Irish Echo*